Explorations in African History:
Reading Patrick Harries

Explorations in African History: Reading Patrick Harries

Edited by
Veit Arlt, Stephanie Bishop, and Pascal Schmid

Basler Afrika Bibliographien

© 2015 Authors and Photographers
© 2015 Basler Afrika Bibliographien

Namibia Resource Centre & Southern Africa Library
Klosterberg 23
PO Box 2037
CH 4051 Basel
Switzerland
www.baslerafrika.ch

CARL SCHLETTWEIN
STIFTUNG

The Basler Afrika Bibliographien is part of the Carl Schlettwein Foundation

Cover photographs:
'M. H. A. Junod à la chasse aux papillons à Shilouvane' (Mr. H. A. Junod chasing butterflies in Shilouvane).
South Africa, ca. 1901–1907. Picture from the collections of the Département Missionnaire Lausanne, held
at the Archives Cantonales Vaudoises (reference number impa-m60241). Copyright DM-échange et mission.
'Human moles follow the compressed air drill—developing a drift in the greatest gold bearing region of the
world, Crown Mine, Johannesburg, S. Africa.' South Africa, ca. 1935. Picture held at the Library of Congress
Prints and Photographs Division Washington, D.C. (reference number LC-USZ62-61383). No known copyright restrictions.

Editors: Veit Arlt, Stephanie Bishop, Pascal Schmid
Proof reading: Stephanie Bishop, Sarah Staehelin
Layout and typesetting: Tilo Richter

ISBN 978-3-905758-62-7

Preface

In 2001, Basel offered various gateways for studying and writing African history. The town had a rich history of contact with the African continent which was manifest in various archives and collections such as those of the Basel Mission, the Basler Afrika Bibliographien, and the Museum der Kulturen, to name just the most important ones. The University of Basel reflected its long-term engagement with the continent in regular courses taught (from 1989) by Paul Jenkins, head archivist of the Basel Mission, and by Albert Wirz and Christoph Marx who, with the support of the Carl Schlettwein Foundation, officiated as guest lecturers (from 1997). The time was ripe to establish African history firmly at the University of Basel and this desire was voiced by both scholars working on Africa and an active group of students.

It was again the Carl Schlettwein Foundation that provided the financial basis for an endowed professorship in African history in 2001. The university sought a historian with a solid track record, a wide international network, and an outstanding reputation who would not only live up to Basel's existing resources and prevailing dynamics in the field of African history but who would also strive to invigorate them and enhance their visibility. They found such a historian in Patrick Harries. Patrick had taught African history at the University of Cape Town, his alma mater, since 1975. After he earned a PhD at the School of Oriental and African Studies (SOAS) at the University of London, Patrick was appointed Associate Professor at the University of Cape Town in 1993. He had a sound international profile on the basis of fellowships at the University of Lausanne, the *École des Hautes Études en Sciences Sociales* (1992) and the *Maison des Sciences de l'Homme* (1996) in Paris, the Humboldt University in Berlin (1996), the *Institut d'Études Politiques de Paris* (2000) and the University of Wisconsin in Madison (2001). He thus collaborated within a broad network of eminent scholars in Africa, the UK and the USA. Patrick's craftsmanship was also gaining notoriety through his published work, including his widely acknowledged monograph *Work, Culture and Identity: Migrant Labour in Mozambique and South Africa, c.1860–1910* (1994).

Patrick joined the University of Basel in 2001, and he challenged and delighted the intellectual community there until his retirement in January 2015. During this period 30 MA and 14 PhD theses were successfully completed under his supervision, and several PhD theses are in their final phase. Many of these theses were part of the research projects Patrick instigated on the history of knowledge, science and medicine, and missionary endeavours. This research focus on the history of knowledge production and Christian missions is also reflected in the publications he authored during his time in Basel, for instance the monograph *Butterflies and Barbarians: Swiss Missionaries and Systems of Knowledge in Southeast Africa* (2007) and the volume *The Spiritual in the Secular: Missionaries and Knowledge about Africa* (2012), which he edited with David Maxwell. Patrick's research and teaching alike established African history as a distinguishing field at the Department of History in Basel and he significantly contributed towards the research and teaching activities at the Centre for African Studies Basel.

In recent years, Patrick's research interests have shifted towards the transatlantic slave trade, the role of the Cape of Good Hope and, in particular, the fate of the African diaspora at the Cape. As an internationally renowned scholar, he was awarded fellowships at *Re:Work* (International Research Centre Work and Human Life Cycle in Global History) at the Humboldt University in Berlin (2010) and a Smuts Visiting Research Fellowship at the University of Cambridge (2011).

Patrick's commitment and spirit, incisive commentary, compelling presentation style and roguish humour have inspired and motivated many colleagues and students. Some of them have contributed to this publication. The authors were invited to reflect on Patrick's œuvre with reference to their own scholarship or vice-versa. Some of the contributions directly address Patrick's books and articles, while others take his teaching, correspondence, remarks or intellectual life more broadly as a point of reference. Some are straightforward academic pieces, while others are personal essays. This collection does not tell the full extent of Patrick's vocation and influence in Basel, of course, but each contribution pays tribute to a brilliant and inspiring scholar, a great teacher, and a kind person.

With Patrick's retirement one necessary and rather dreary part of his work has come to an end—he is now delivered from managerial and administrative tasks. This frees time for Patrick to concentrate on activities that are his particular passion: research and exchange. Another prestigious fellowship accordingly marks the next step in his career as a scholar. In the first half of 2015, he is concentrating on his research on the slave trade and the Cape's "Mozbieker" community at the *Institut d'Études Avancées* in Nantes. Wherever his future work takes him, we are confident Patrick's insights will continue to enrich the field of African history, and scholarship in Basel in particular. We wish him many fruitful and joyful chapters yet to come.

Acknowledgements

We would like to thank the contributors as well as all those who helped to make this publication possible: Lorena Rizzo, Giorgio Miescher, Dag Henrichsen and Cassandra Mark for conceptualisation, administration and fundraising; Benjamin Brühwiler, Jon Schubert, Sarah Staehelin, Henri-Michel Yéré as well as several of the authors for providing peer-review and corrections; Petra Kerkhoff and her team at the BAB publishing house for their advice and patience.

Last but not least we would like to thank the Carl Schlettwein Foundation for its generous financial support for this volume, but even more importantly, for its investment in African History and African Studies at the University of Basel.

Basel, May 2015
Veit Arlt, Stephanie Bishop, and Pascal Schmid

Eric Morier-Genoud

The Making of a Transnational Historian: Patrick Harries in Lausanne

Patrick Harries spent a year in Switzerland in 1991–1992. This constitutes a short and little-known episode in his long career. It is an important moment however, because it marked a turning point in Patrick's intellectual trajectory. This is when and where Patrick operated a shift from social history to cultural history and from an Africanist standpoint to a more connected historical approach. Said differently, Lausanne 1991–92 is a turning point in Patrick becoming a transnational historian of culture along the lines later formalised by Fred Cooper and Ann Stoler in their volume *Tensions of Empire*.[1]

Patrick came to Switzerland in 1991 as a visiting professor at the University of Lausanne. He was invited to substitute professor François Jequier, an economic historian specialised in the question of watch manufacturing in Switzerland, who was going on sabbatical. Patrick taught two modules in Lausanne lasting the whole academic year (as it used to be in those pre-Bologna days), namely a seminar on South African history ('L'Afrique du Sud: un pays divisé') and an ex-catedra course on Europeans' views of the African continent ('Une histoire culturelle de l'Afrique'). As part of these courses, Patrick invited David Birmingham to give a lecture about the history of Angola and Alpheus Manghezi to present the method of oral history as he practised it in Mozambique.

I was a student at the University of Lausanne in 1991 doing a BA in political science. Due to my interest in Africa, I sat in the two modules which Patrick offered and thus experienced his unique teaching approach and motivation. Drawing on the British tradition, Patrick demanded that we not only make presentations, but also run the seminar discussions. At the first session, he explained that the aim was not just to acquire new information, but also to acquire a capacity to make arguments and defend our own point of view—that is, to develop a sense of critique and improve our debating skills. Outside the classroom, Patrick was very approachable and he held regular office hours, something which was unusual in Lausanne; students thus met and talked to him at length about their essays, their studies and their futures.

In Lausanne, Patrick assembled around him a group of students and teaching assistants who had an interest in Africa, and he encouraged them to do original research in missionary archives (of the Mission Romande and the Philafrican Mission). With Patrick's support, and under the direction of Klauspeter Blaser, a professor of theology with teaching experience in South Africa (at the Federal Theological Seminary in Alice), these students went on to launch the publication

Le Fait Missionnaire (LFM) which, from being an irregular publication in 1995, grew to become the peer-reviewed journal *Social Sciences and Missions*.[2] In its first years, LFM published several revised BA Hons and MA theses, four of which were from students close to Patrick in Lausanne: Nicolas Monnier, Didier Péclard, Martina Egli, and the author of this text.

Patrick had been to Switzerland before 1991. His first visit had taken place seven years earlier, in 1984–1985, when he came as a post-doctoral fellow to work in the archives of the Mission Romande (housed in the *Département missionnaire des églises de la Suisse Romande*). These archives held rich material about the Tsonga/Shangaan people who lived in South Africa and Mozambique and who Patrick studied. During his time in Lausanne, Patrick took an intensive course in French at the University of Fribourg and thus drastically improved the little French he had learned earlier during a short visit to France before studying for his BA in Cape Town. While in Lausanne in 1985–86 Patrick also took part in the activities of the Vaudois branch of the Swiss Anti-Apartheid Movement (MAA). It was at an MAA meeting in 1985 that he met his wife Isabelle Vauthier who was to decisively shape his understanding of Swiss culture and Swiss Romande history.

In 1991–92 Patrick had not yet published his great work of social history *Work, Culture and Identity*.[3] Yet he was already shifting to cultural history and to a more connected historical approach. Patrick's courses at the University of Lausanne illustrate this: one module was about Africa, looking at South Africa from an African perspective, while the other module looked at the European views of Africa, unpacking the long history of the European understandings of the "dark continent" (focusing on the idea of race, the theory and practice of museums, etc.). Similarly Patrick's research in the archives was no longer just concerned with Africans but also with Switzerland and Swiss missionaries, not least the famous Henri Alexandre Junod. This new interest in Swiss history led Patrick to delve into his father-in-law's private library. Isabelle's father (son and grandson of Free Church pastors and Vaudois patriots) had indeed kept the family's rich library where Patrick read Swiss Francophone classics such as Eugène Rambert and Henri Vuilleumier.

Patrick's stay in Lausanne took place in a singular historical context. Switzerland in 1991–92 was embroiled in a profound identity crisis. The Berlin wall had collapsed and Swiss citizens had just discovered that a third of the population had been spied on for decades by a federal police who looked suspiciously at anyone not opposed to communism. The government had secretly bought property abroad so as to flee should the country be invaded, and it had set up a secret parallel structure within the army (known as P-26) to bypass formal (and democratic) authority lines. A vivid debate was also under way about the nature of Switzerland's neutrality during the Second World War. These discoveries and debates shattered many myths and led Swiss citizens to question themselves and search for a new way to look at their history and identity. Patrick lived through this period intensively, reading the literary production of the moment and debating the situation with colleagues, friends and students. This influenced his thinking and his own work on identity, whether Swiss or African—see for example his 1998 article 'Missionary Endeavour and the Politics of Identity in Switzerland'.[4]

Patrick has continued to visit Lausanne after 1992 to do research, to visit his in-laws and his daughter who did her BA at the University of Lausanne, and to see friends. Isabelle says Patrick has become very fond of Lausanne, loving the city for its quietness, its views, and its old town—presumably in addition to of its archives and university. The big question, to my mind, is whether Lausanne was just a (nice) place (like any other) where Patrick happened to operate a major intellectual shift or whether Lausanne actually shaped this scholar's transformation? Indeed what was the influence of Isabelle, of Patrick's in-laws, and of Lausanne's academia on Patrick intellectual transformation? I cannot reasonably answer this question here, except to say that there has been some influence—probably more than we realise. Whatever the extent, what can and should be said more firmly is that the outcome of Patrick's personal Swiss-South African encounter has enriched the Swiss and South African historiographies, the transnational historical approach, and Patrick's many friends, colleagues and students.

1   Fred Cooper and Ann Stoler, eds. *Tensions of Empire: Colonial Cultures in a Bourgeois World* (Berkeley: University of California Press, 1998).

2   *Social Sciences and Missions* (Leiden: Brill), www.brill.nl/ssm.

3   Patrick Harries, *Work, Culture and Identity: Migrant Laborers in Mozambique and South Africa, C. 1860–1910* (Portsmouth, NH: Heinemann, 1994).

4   Patrick Harries, 'Missionary Endeavour and the Politics of Identity in Switzerland', *Le Fait Missionnaire*, 6 (1988): 39–69.

Pascal Schmid

From Swiss Imperialism to Postcolonial Switzerland

In 1998, a special issue of the Swiss history journal *Traverse* asked: 'Is there a Swiss imperialism?'[1] A few years later, this rhetorical question had become obsolete as far as academic discussions were concerned. It was answered not only by the editors and authors of the 1998 *Traverse* issue, but also by other scholarly work produced about Switzerland's role in the colonial world and the importance of the colonial world for the history of Switzerland. Some of this work contributed towards a conference that took place in Basel in 2003. In a way, the title of the conference referred to the question of the existence of a Swiss imperialism: 'Imperial Culture in Countries without Colonies: Africa and Switzerland'. The title also indicated a shift of focus or, rather, widening of the scope beyond an economic and political understanding of imperialism, by emphasising culture.

It was the first major conference Patrick Harries organised in Basel, and it also offered the frame for the general assembly of the Swiss Society for African Studies (SSEA) that year. The conference marked the significance of African history for Basel and Switzerland on the one hand; on the other hand, it highlighted the importance of cultural history and postcolonial thinking for both the history of Africa and of Switzerland. The event was also a milestone in my own academic and professional career. Patrick hired me as a student assistant and offered me the opportunity to get involved in both the intellectual and, in particular, the logistic dimensions of mounting a scientific conference. In both dimensions I learned a lot.

The event brought together established scholars from Africa and Europe as well as younger researchers from Basel and Switzerland (some of whom have contributed chapters to this volume). It connected local researchers and their work with a transnational academic network—something that was to remain an important aspect of Patrick's scholarship in Basel. The conference adumbrated his future efforts to bring an impressive number of eminent scholars to Basel, and his contribution to putting Basel on the map as a centre for academic engagement with African history and Africa more generally.

The conference contributions were about travellers, soldiers, scientists, activists, merchants and—of course—missionaries. It focused on an imperial culture formed and embodied by mainly Swiss actors who were driven by, as the conference description says, 'geographical curiosity, cartography, anti-slavery agitation, commercial enterprise [including, in particular, investment in the trans-Atlantic slave trade] and scientific interest...[as well as] by evangelical enthusiasm'. The conference was to 'examine the extent to which Swiss history was made in the corners of the European world. At the same time, it [would] look at the contribution of Swiss societies and individuals to the history of that part of the world that is Africa'. Especially the first part of this claim was path-breaking and ambitious, as it referred to the examination of how Africa contributed 'to the modernity produced in Europe during the late nineteenth and twentieth centuries'. Contributors were called upon to look into the 'vibrant images of Africa that were carried into many Swiss homes' and at how these images 'served to define and reinforce Swiss ideas about politics, morality, generosity, frugality and civic virtue'.[2]

The conference certainly amplified and intensified discussions about these questions and sensitised many young and maybe also more senior scholars for its cause. The conference marked a step from the examination of a Swiss imperialism focused on economic and political issues to a more cultural-oriented approach—one that examines "Postcolonial Switzerland", as the editors of a volume of the same title explained almost a decade later. For them, such an approach would 'beyond the economic and political entanglements refer to Swiss everyday life, science and popular cultures by paying particular attention to representation, imagination, the discursive and the visual'.[3] Many papers presented at the 2003 conference managed to do so in amazingly innovative ways.

Unfortunately, the conference contributions were not published as an edited volume or special issue of a journal. And the conference website that had made the original conference papers accessible to a wider public is no longer online. However, numerous contributions can be found in revised, extended, or sharpened form. Many of them fed into journal articles or contributions in edited volumes, such as Guy Thomas' examination of spatial transformation in colonial Cameroon;[4] Patrick Minder's analysis of human exhibitions in the 1890s and 1920s;[5] the paper by Marcel Dreier, who examined how the identity of the Swiss solidarity group *Kämpfendes Afrika* was formed by the relationship and exchange with African liberation movements;[6] or Erika Eichholzer's discussion of the use (and abuse) of Twi citations in mission magazines, which was taken up in her contribution to the volume *The Spiritual in the Secular* (co-edited by Patrick).[7]

Some papers drew on research that was later expanded to become theses and monographs such as those by Giorgio Miescher,[8] Ulrike Sill,[9] Daniel Gilfoyle[10] and Hans Fässler.[11] Tim Couzens critically reviewed his own biography of the Swiss missionary Édouard Jaccottet,[12] while Bothlale Tema reflected on her ancestors' encounter with another missionary, Henri Gonin, which was an important element of her autobiographic novel.[13] Other presentations informed specific chapters in monographs or theses, for instance Monica Kalt's discussion of the anti-imperialist discourse of advocacy and solidarity organizations in Switzerland in the 1970s,[14] or the examination of abolition agitation (against the trans-Atlantic slave trade) and anti-slavery movements (focusing on slavery in Africa) in Switzerland in the nineteenth century by Bouda Etemad and David Thomas (two of the editors of the *Traverse* issue mentioned previously) as well as Janick Schaufelbuehl.[15]

Patrick himself presented a discussion of the images of Africa and Africans conveyed by Sunday schools in western, French-speaking Switzerland from the 1860s to the 1920s. He suggested that contact with Africa as it took place in the frame of the Sunday schools 'helped the Swiss to define their sense of identity on a vision of themselves as a particularly humane and civilized people'. He pointed to the 'inevitably dark side to this story of generosity and achievement', when he argued that the 'evangelical views of Africa played an important role in creating the cultural conditions of racism and imperialism'. The paper partly fed into the chapter 'African Itineraries & Swiss Identities' of his acclaimed monograph *Butterflies and Barbarians,* to which, obviously, the theme of the conference formed the context.[16]

I had participated in several seminars and lectures with Patrick before, including a study trip to South Africa.[17] I knew him as a person and teacher, and I had read some of his work. But by organising and witnessing the conference, I got to know Patrick as a scholar. I may not have realised this during the preparation for, or even through attending the conference. Certainly, he had imparted some of his ideas on history and historiography to his students in class. And I remember having had insightful discussions with Patrick about the work and papers of the participants and the structuring of the panels before the conference. But only in the course of time did it occur to me that I really got to know Patrick as a scholar—the significance of his scholarship—by engaging in an event that represents a landmark in the study of African (and, yes, global) history in Basel and Switzerland.

At the time, the ideas that were propagated by the conference and discussed during its panels—a postcolonial perspective and a culturally informed social history—seemed naturally to be part of my studies in African history. Only later did I realise that they were part of something that was emerging and developing at the time. It was the first major conference to examine the cultural history of colonial or imperial Switzerland, at least according to my knowledge and discussions with colleagues. Patrick played a crucial role in bringing these ideas to the research site Basel—and in making them part of the common historiographical repertoire of undergraduate students like me.

Imperial Culture in Countries without Colonies: Africa and Switzerland
23–25 October 2003, Basel, Switzerland

Conference panels and presentations

Intellectuals: Missionaries, Anthropology and Linguistics

David Coplan: A Grand Quixotic Intellectual Quest: Western Switzerland and Missionary Anthropology in 19th Century Lesotho

Tom McCaskie: Perregaux among the Akan

David Birmingham & Didier Péclard: Héli Chatelain and the Colonial Encounter in Angola

Erika Eichholzer: Language and Misrepresentation: Swiss Missionary Linguists and the Non-European Other

Alain Ricard: The Ellenbergers (David-Frederic, Victor, Paul): Interpreting Sesotho

Intellectuals: Between Science and Romance

Nigel Penn & Roland Kaehr: Gen. Charles-Daniel de Meuron at the Cape and in Switzerland

Wolbert Smidt: A Swiss in Africa: Munzinger between Scholarship, Political Reform and Imperialism

Bernhard Gardi: René Gardi (1909–2000): Traveller, Writer, Photographer and Filmmaker

William Beinart & Daniel Gilfoyle: A Swiss Vet in South Africa: Arnold Theiler, the South African Stock Industry and the Lamsiekte Problem

Giorgio Miescher: From Rinderpest to the Basel Zoo. Markus Zschokke or How Vets, Monuments and Nature Conservation Opened a Line against Dark Africa

Science and Exploration

Guy Thomas: Spatial Transformation in Colonial Cameroon: Cantons, Chiefdoms and Missionary Cartography

Werner Korte: Expeditions into an Unknown Country: The Journeys of Johann A. Büttikofer through Liberia in the Years 1880–1882 and 1886

Dag Henrichsen: Classifying Colonial Territory and Mapping out an Academic Career: The Example of Hans Schinz, Botanist in South-Western Africa and Zurich

Jürg Schneider: Photographs and Findings: Carl Passavant's Travelling and Exploring in West Africa

Institutions and Intellectuals

Paul Jenkins: What is a Missionary Society? A Systematic View of a Key Institution in Imperial and Post-Imperial Culture

Ulrike Sill & Sara Janner: From India via Basel to the Gold Coast. The Basel Women's Mission in the Nineteenth Century

Eric Morier-Genoud: Missionary Mismatch: H. P. Junod's Politics in South Africa and Switzerland, ca. 1930–1980s

Cephas Omenyo: The Legacies of the Basel Mission in Ghana Revisited

Alpheus Manghesi: Out of Bounds: Control, Discipline and Passive Resistance in a Mission College

Africa in Switzerland/Servitude and Freedom

Wolbert Smidt: Africans in Switzerland: The Example of Basel in the 19th Century

Patrick Minder: Le 'zoo humain' en Suisse, objet de curiosité populaire ou instrument de propagande coloniale?

Patrick Harries: Taming Domestic Savages: The Image of Africa in Sunday Schools of Western Switzerland, ca. 1860–1960

Hans Fässler: The Third Chapter is the First: Unravelling Switzerland's Slavery Past

Botlhale Tema: Henri Gonin and Welgeval Farm: From Servitude to Salvation

Christianity and Transculturation

Sonia Abun-Nasr: Patterns of Life: Christian Biographies from Switzerland and Ghana

Tim Couzens: Edward Jacottet and the Development of an Indigenous Pastorate in Lesotho

Gaby Fierz: Swiss African Chief and Queenmother: Auf den Spuren transkultureller Identitäten

African Images and Swiss Indentities

Bouda Etemad & Thomas David: Mouvements abolitionnistes et valeurs culturelles : Le cas de la Suisse

Marcel Dreier: Africa is Fighting: A Swiss Anti-Imperialist Solidarity Movement and Its Models of Liberation in the 1970s

Monica Kalt: 'Entwicklung heisst Befreiung': Kritisches entwicklungspolitisches Engagement in der Schweiz der 70er und 80er Jahre

1   Thomas David and Bouda Etemad, 'Gibt es einen schweizerischen Imperialismus? Zur Einführung', *Traverse*, no. 2 (1998): 7–27.

2   'Imperial Culture in Countries without Colonies: Africa and Switzerland' (Conference Programme), 2003

3   Patricia Purtschert, Barbara Lüthi, and Francesca Falk, 'Eine Bestandesaufnahme der postkolonialen Schweiz', in *Postkoloniale Schweiz: Formen und Folgen eines Kolonialismus ohne Kolonien*, ed. Patricia Purtschert, Barbara Lüthi, and Francesca Falk (Bielefeld: transcript Verlag, 2012), 30. In a footnote on the same page, the authors refer to the conference as a 'first attempt' to answer such questions.

4   Guy Thomas, 'Chiefdoms, Cantons, and Contentious Land: Mapping out a Mission Field in Twentieth Century Colonial Cameroon', in *Christianity and Social Change in Africa: Essays in Honor of J.D.Y. Peel*, ed. Toyin Falola (Durham: Carolina Academic Press, 2005), 517–48.

5   Patrick Minder, 'Les zoos humains en Suisse', in *Zoos humains et exhibitions coloniales : 150 ans d'invention de l'Autre*, ed. N. Bancel et al. (Paris: La Découverte, 2012), 361–72.

6   Marcel Dreier, 'Afrikanische Befreiungsbewegungen und die antiimperialistische Solidaritätsbewegung in der Schweiz', in *1968–1978: Ein bewegtes Jahrzehnt in der Schweiz*, ed. Janick Marina Schaufelbuehl and Nuno Pereira (Zürich: Chronos, 2009), 161–76.

7   Erika Eichholzer, 'Missionary Linguistics on the Gold Coast: Wristling with Language', in *The Spiritual in the Secular: Missionaries and Knowledge about Africa*, ed. Patrick Harries and David Maxwell (Grand Rapids: Wm. B. Eerdmans Publishing, 2012), 72–99.

8   Giorgio Miescher, *Namibia's Red Line: The History of a Veterinary and Settlement Border* (New York: Palgrave Macmillan, 2012).

9   Ulrike Sill, *Encounters in Quest of Christian Womanhood: The Basel Mission in Pre- and Early Colonial Ghana* (Leiden: Brill, 2010).

10   Daniel Gilfoyle and Karen Brown, *Frontiers of Knowledge: Veterinary Science, Environment and the State in South Africa, 1900–1950* (Saarbrücken: VDM Verlag Dr. Müller, 2010).

11   Hans Fässler, *Reise in Schwarz-Weiß: Schweizer Ortstermine in Sachen Sklaverei* (Zürich: Rotpunktverlag, 2006).

12   Tim Couzens, *Murder at Morija: Faith, Mystery, and Tragedy on an African Mission* (Charlottesville: University Press of Virginia, 2005).

13   Botlhale Tema, *The People Of Welgeval* (Cape Town: Struik Publishers, 2006).

14   Monica Kalt, *Tiersmondismus in der Schweiz der 1960er und 1970er Jahre: Von der Barmherzigkeit zur Solidarität* (Bern: Peter Lang, 2010).

15   Thomas David, Bouda Etemad, and Janick Marina Schaufelbuehl, *La Suisse et L'esclavage des Noirs* (Lausanne: Ed. Antipodes, 2005); Thomas David, Bouda Etemad, and Janick Marina Schaufelbuehl, *Schwarze Geschäfte* (Zürich: Limmat Verlag, 2005).

16   Patrick Harries, *Butterflies & Barbarians: Swiss Missionaries and Systems of Knowledge in South-East Africa* (Oxford: Ohio University Press, 2007), 35–66. The theme is also taken up in a book chapter: Patrick Harries, 'Dompter les sauvages domestiques : le rôle de l'Afrique dans les Ecoles du dimanche en Suisse romande, 1860–1920', in *Suisse – Afrique (18e–20e siècles) : de la traite des Noirs à la fin du régime de l'apartheid*, ed. Sandra Bott and Thomas David (Münster: LIT, 2005), S. 227–46.

17   In August 2002, a group of around ten history students from the University of Basel spent three weeks on a field excursion in the Limpopo Province.

Dag Henrichsen

Hildagonda Duckitt's (and Patrick Harries')
Contribution to Namibian History

When Patrick took up his position at the Department of History at the University of Basel he brought with him a fascinating network of scholars, scholarship and themes and greatly advanced the internationalisation of African history teaching and researching in Basel. At the Basler Afrika Bibliographien (BAB), since 1995 the Namibia Resource Centre and Southern Africa Library, this internationalisation was felt instantly. Whilst Patrick conceded at one stage that the BAB made him feel at home in Basel, he conversely supported our attempts to feel at home in the wider network of African archives, libraries and research. He surprised some of us by his extensive knowledge of the entangled relations between Switzerland and Southern Africa. Shortly after his arrival he put the research question of "Imperial Culture in countries without Colonies" and its relevance to Swiss history squarely at our doorstep. We in turn seem to have surprised him, as so many South African historians, with our insistence on framing Namibia as "the heart of the matter". We insisted particularly on the relevance of South Africa's colony Namibia for South African history and historiography. He did, of course, share our understanding of the paradigmatic negligence in South African historiography of South Africa's colonial history in the region and South African historians' inward-looking tendencies. He often reminded us, for example during the opening workshop in 2009 on 'The South African Empire?' of his own battles, in South Africa, to push for African histories beyond South Africa's national borders. At South African universities, he explained, his interests in Mozambican history and southeastern African themes and networks at times created a sense of marginality. In part, then, Patrick's coming to Basel deepened and broadened questions in Basel which are vexing African historiography and European imperial history to this day. These questions all relate to the various frameworks of nationalism, their academic canons and institutions.

Patrick staunchly supported the many Namibia-related teaching and research projets developing at the BAB. Yet, he stuck to the broader views and themes, as such reminding some of us more implicitly than explicitly of the trappings of our nationalist framework. His interest in our personal research projects and in our advancement as scholars and our Namibian network was one in which he was attentive to detail.

A note from him dating from early 2007 is a typical example. Patrick alerted me to Hildagonda Duckitt's *Diary of a Cape Housekeeper*, published in London in 1902, and in it the brief mentioning of Damara women selling vegetables in Cape Town in the late nineteenth century. I was at the time researching the labour relations between central Namibia and the Cape colony in the nineteenth century, a virtually unknown history which targeted Damara communities in particular. Damara were indentured in their hundreds, men, women and children, on farms and in households at the Cape in the late 1870s and early 1880s. At that time Patrick had immersed himself into slave and labour relations between the Cape and southeastern Africa and was focused on the highly cosmopolitan African labour market at the Cape.

Duckitt had lived in Plumstead and Wynberg at the Cape since 1888 and her book 'was intended to help young women, particularly those born overseas, to run their modest South African homes efficiently and economically'.[1] Visualising an ideal daily routine for her readership she wrote that 'the butcher comes for orders, and often a cart calls bringing vegetables, or the Damara women living at Constantia bring baskets of greens to your kitchen door'.[2] Whilst this snippet of evidence on Damara women and their apparent economic niche at the Cape entered my essay,[3] Patrick added two typical suggestions to the brief email correspondence which followed his note: 'The book is very well-known in SA. I hope the BAB has a copy'. BAB did not have a copy but saw to it to get one immediately. And he suggested that I contact the Cape Argus columnist Jackie Loos who had written about Duckitt's cookery books in that newspaper before. As it turned out, Loos herself was interested in the Cape labour export history from central Namibia.

Cookery and cook books are a fascinating, though often neglected historical source. The renowned Swiss historian Albert Wirz had put the subject of 'the colonial kitchen' on the research agenda with his pioneering essay 'Essen und Herrschen. Zur Ethnographie der kolonialen Küche in Kamerun vor 1914' ('Eating and ruling. On the Ethnography of the Colonial Kitchen in Cameroon before 1914'), published in 1984 in the likewise renowned journal at the time Genève-Afrique. BAB did acquire a couple of German colonial cook books in the mid-1990s but, given our Namibia focus, we failed to look beyond its borders. It thus took Patrick for this to happen. I hasten to say that he also suggested many other titles of monographs and periodicals apart from Duckitt's diary for acquisition. His engagement with Namibian history of course did not end with Duckitt's diary. By 2007 he was supervising two Namibian students in Basel, Martha Akawa and Timo Mashuna, apart from a number of other PhD and MA theses on Namibian history such as Lorena Rizzo's, Giorgio Miescher's, Anna Vögeli's or Luregn Lenggenhager's theses. His record with regard to Namibian history is solid!

1   Jackie Loos, 'Cape Housekeeping', *Cape Argus*, December 29, 2004.
2   In Hildagonda Duckitt, *Hilda's Diary of a Cape Housekeeper* (London: 1978; Facsimile Reprint), 30.
3   Dag Henrichsen, '"Damara" Labour Recruitment to the Cape Colony and Marginalization and Hegemony in Late 19th Century Central Namibia,' *Journal of Namibian Studies*, 3 (2008): 63–82.

Rita Kesselring

Cultural Reproduction and Memory: Past, Present and Future

In this essay, I reflect on the relationships between historical analysis and social anthropology, and memory and cultural reproduction. I argue that anthropology has not entirely overcome a functionalist notion of society, and thereby fails to fully understand cultural reproduction. This has resulted in a continuous disciplinary separation between history and anthropology. By reviewing the debates on social change in Southern Africa, I will offer an avenue to a shared project between the two disciplines on the study of social change.

In a rather critical essay, Max Gluckman[1] expressed his disappointment about Malinowski's analysis of social change. Malinowski's blindness for the driving forces of social change, Gluckman argues, comes from his assumption that culture is static. Culture is either European or African and, if the two come into contact, a third—separate—'cultural reality' emerges, a zone of contact and change. For Malinowski, 'each of these orders is subject to a specific determinism of its own'.[2]

Conversely, Gluckman's research approach as followed during his engagement at the Rhodes Livingstone Institute (RLI) and later as professor in Manchester was formed under the premise that the 'African man' is capable of modernity, because living conditions shape culture. As he stated it in his famous formula: 'An African townsman is a townsman, an African miner is a miner'.[3] He and his colleagues did not deny that ethnicity and tribal affiliations continue to play a role, but argued that the interaction between tribal typologies and urban realities should be seen as happening within one 'single social field'.

Accordingly, Gluckman interprets what happens to men when they leave their home villages to work in the mines as an ordinary process that could be observed in any capitalist society: 'If we conceive the tribal and urban areas to be one social field, we say that as soon as an African moves from a reserve to an urban area he is "detribalized" in the sense that he comes under White authority without his chief, he works in different ways, he associates with different types of individuals, &c. But he is still tribalized, for of course he does not cease to be influenced by tribal culture'.[4]

Gluckman and his colleagues at the RLI were aware that the meaning of 'tradition' changed as it entered the industrial setting, and what one could observe were at best fragments of the past or the lived tribal system in the rural areas. For instance, James Clyde Mitchell took the 'tribal' Kalela dance 'as a vehicle for a general enquiry into tribalism and some other features of social relationships among Africans in the towns'.[5] However, Philip Mayer[6] criticised them from a South African perspective in that they drew conclusions on the tribal system of knowledge by observing its reconstruction and reinterpretation in the urban settings.

The RLI scholars adhered to a structural functionalism which explained individual behaviour in terms of more or less clearly demarcated cultural and social systems of norms and knowledge, 'two entirely different domains of knowledge, more or less understood as analogous to two stages of social evolution and thus legitimately requiring different explanatory models'.[7] In the late colonial period, a new generation of researchers broke away from functionalism. In their network studies, they adopted an individual-centred approach by focusing on the personal relationships an individual entertained and the nature of these contacts.[8] Even if these networks often straddle the urban and the rural, researchers clearly privileged the experience of urbanity rather than the home villages.[9]

The RLI and Manchester School studies clearly produced landmark studies in urban anthropology. They were guided by the question of how society reproduces itself. When scholars asked about the shifts in subjectivities people undergo as they become migrant workers, it was really an inquiry into the role past practices and forms of sociality play in a different social, political and economic context. Formulated more to the point: what is it that prevents a society from breaking apart when its members become urban and modern?

Cultural reproduction and memory

The question of cultural reproduction lies at the heart of the anthropological project. It seemed easy to answer it for "traditional" societies—somehow, the same cultural elements were silently passed on from generation to generation. But what happens when traditions obviously break? Melville Herskovits, as early as the 1930s, asked about West African cultural elements in the Afro-American life-worlds, 'What do the Africans do that the inhabitants of the Negro quarter in New York also do?'[10] Like most of his contemporaries, he accepted some racial determinism in the survival of certain practices; however, he tended to be more sympathetic towards some kind of cultural conditioning. He rejected the dominant thinking at the time that slaves had lost all traces of their past by the rupture of enslavement. Patrick Harries describes missionary and anthropologist Henri Junod's perspective on black mineworkers on the early Witwatersrand Gold Mines in a similar way: 'stripped of sustaining a culture'.[11]

The question of cultural reproduction today is somewhat lost in anthropological theory—or rather hidden in the more fashionable notion of "memory". The "memory boom" in the humanities and the social sciences during the 1990s was helpful to view memory as more than a set of representations of events or experiences. Today, scholars speak of multiple pasts and multiple memories[12] and they generally agree that memory persists because people act in and upon a world of discourse, meaning and sociality. As Maurice Halbwachs[13] noted already in the 1920s, we construct the past by remembering, and our present concerns determine what part of the past we shall remember.

But what role does memory really play in social reproduction? We still lack a clear conceptualization of how what is being remembered (cognitively or not) produces continuity or change. As Johannes Fabian states, the 'concept of memory may become indistinguishable from either identity or culture';[14] and David Berliner fears that the 'conceptual extension [of the notion of memory] lead[s] to the entanglement of memory and culture'.[15] Apart from conflating memory and cultural change, current scholarship often resorts to the discursive, representational level when establishing the (all too causal) link between something of the past and current practice. In the remaining part of this contribution, I conceptually distinguish memory and social change and analyse how the former may lead to the latter. To illustrate my approach, I draw on most recent changes in the Zambian Copperbelt and the adjacent North-western Province.

Changes in the old and new Copperbelt, Zambia

Urban life in the Copperbelt has changed profoundly since the classic Manchester School studies of the Copperbelt and since James Ferguson's[16] seminal study in the 1980s. Since the late 1990s, mines have been privatised and mechanised. The state has little capacity to regulate the extractive industry. The mines employ very few workers. The urban majority pursues mine-related activities, participates in the informal business sector, and resorts to all kinds of subsistence activities. These changes have had huge effects on the figuration of the urban and the rural. The currently booming extractive industry transforms villages into towns and lets new urban structures emerge in the "New Copperbelt", the Northwestern Province.

Against the background of these recent developments in the Zambian mining sector and urban landscape, I now turn to two issues of cultural reproduction the RLI researchers were concerned with at the time: the rural/urban continuum and the urban (built) environment, thereby approximating a conception of memory.

The production of habitual knowledge

The RLI researchers mostly saw migration as a one-way street to the urban area.[17] In current Zambia, though, we witness as much out-migration as in-migration. We can therefore study the transfer of practices both ways, from the rural to the urban and from the urban and the rural. There are numerous practices that people pursue in both settings such as (mechanised and artisanal) mining, farming (urban gardening and agriculture) and construction (houses and infrastructure) to mention but a few. In order to understand the translation and transfer of knowledge across space and time, I suggest focusing on the kind of knowledge people hold that is largely embodied and that they have acquired in engagement with particular forms of sociality and in specific environments. As such we would not assume the existence of a social structure or several social structures but instead explore the transfer of forms of sociality and practices in a 'field habitually traversed by migrating persons'.[18]

Researchers at the RLI and the Manchester School attributed some relevance to the urban set-up. They were rather helpless, however, in capturing the relation between built environment and personhood. I suggest that we internalize the (built) environment around us in the sense that it guides the possibilities for the socialities we live.[19] This process results in habitual knowledge about the world, which conversely influences the social figurations we partake in. When people move to a new built context, they do not lose their "identity" or "culture". They bring along their habituated perception of the world and through it gradually change the new environment. The sedimented knowledge about the "old" environment is the condition for the engagement with the "new" environment.

The subjectivities resulting from these practices of mobility and the lived experience of the urban space are complex. They are, however, not "fragmented" (as post-structuralist suggest) nor can they be conceptualized as separate (as Malinowski suggests). People integrate different forms of sociality into one personhood and act in one life-world. Gluckman, as elaborated above, saw this back-and-forth (or 'alternation') as switching between two distinct systems. If we see it as "changing culture" (for lack of a better word)—of course without falling back to seeing it as a one-way and evolutionary movement from a tribal condition to complete detribalization (as Malinowski suggested)—, we may become attentive to the gradual shifts in subjectivities and practices. How can this be done practically and conceptually?

The productive dimension of memory

From a phenomenological perspective, culture is a part of our sedimented knowledge about the world. What we experience is being integrated into our everyday perception of the world.[20] Through practices that people undertake while engaging within specific environments, a productive kind of knowledge emerges. The results are 'habit memories',[21] which are not only potential but always operative. This operative or, as I would call it, *productive* dimension of memory is manifest in ordinary practices.

Memory is knowledge that is manifest in ordinary practices; it *produces* practices. Given that the major part of that knowledge is embodied and non-predicated,[22] the body is an important site from which social change emerges. This answers the practical question: one important "tangible" way in which we can access the emergence of subjectivities is by observing and participating in practices.

Fitful cultural reproduction

I suggest that the productive dimension of memory is not only manifest in practices but is also the condition for the possibility of social change. Understanding practices as the manifestation of memory results in a study of social change that embraces both the spatial and temporal.[23] Because 'history is operative in [people's] social life',[24] anthropologists have always recorded history even though they primarily worked in and on the present. For instance, a retrenched miner will translate his knowledge acquired in hundreds of hours of mechanised extractive work to an informal small-scale mining setting where he searches for copper in a dump with a pick and a shovel.

The integration of experiences into one's perception of the world does not necessarily entail smooth reproduction, though, for as Hastrup writes, 'memory is far from mechanical'.[25] We can think of instances of violence or sudden changes in the environment. When a miner moves from the paternalistically designed old Copperbelt town Kitwe to Lumwana, currently a mine camp in the Northwestern Province, the new environment demands a quite different form of bodily navigation—just as miners moving between rural and urban areas in the 1940s had to integrate different forms of sociality into their everyday being-in-the-world.

These are moments when memory and current practice seem not to fit. The moments when people "stumble" give us clues about the possibility of emancipation from a system.[26] Hence, processes of habituation do not only reproduce society (as Bourdieu[27] shows); they are also a source of change.[28]

History and anthropology

In conclusion, I would widen Isaac Schapera's restricted view of the anthropologist's capacity to 'provide material for future historians by giving a detailed account of the social condition of the people at the time of his fieldwork'[29] by the anthropologist's capacity to indeed witness social change as it unfolds. Even through Evans-Pritchard lashed out against Malinowski, the functionalists and their 'desire to keep up with the Joneses, the natural scientists', his statement on the similarities between history and social anthropology still ring true today: 'Social anthropology and history are both branches of social science, or social studies, and [...] consequently there is an overlap of relevance between them and each can learn much from one another'.[30] Historians and anthropologists cannot only work complementarily with a clear division of labour but they can actually work *together*.

While I agree with Godfrey Wilson's and Monica Hunter's concern (who were confronted with the lack of written records on pre-colonial African society) that 'every society is always changing, and unless we can probe the change some way back we cannot properly understand it',[31] in this essay, I argued in the line of Marshall Sahlins who does not see a phenomenological reason to juxtapose history and structure nor stability and change: 'Every practical change is also a cultural reproduction. [...] Every reproduction of culture is an alteration'.[32] Cultural reproduction, and therefore social change, happens through embodied knowledge. I tried to show that a more phenomenological approach to cultural reproduction and what persists (memory) would bring anthropology closer to an historical analysis of society and thereby closer to a shared project with history.

1 Max Gluckman, 'Malinowski's "Functional" Analysis of Social Change', *Africa: Journal of the International African Institute* 17, no. 2 (1947): 103–21.

2 Bronislaw Malinowski, *The Dynamics of Culture Change: An Inquiry into Race Relations in Africa* (New Haven and London: Yale University Press, 1945), 64.

3 Max Gluckman, 'Anthropological Problems Arising from the African Industrial Revolution', in *Social Change in Modern Africa*, ed. A. Southall (London: Oxford University Press, 1961), 69.

4 Gluckman, 'Malinowski's "Functional" Analysis of Social Change', 114.

5 James Clyde Mitchell, *The Kalela Dance: Aspects of Social Relationships Among Urban Africans in Northern Rhodesia* (Manchester: Manchester University Press for Rhodes-Livingstone Institute, 1956), 1.

6 Philip Mayer, 'Migrancy and the Study of Africans in Towns', *American Anthropologist* 64, no. 3 (1962): 576–92.

7 Sally Falk Moore, *Anthropology and Africa: Changing Perspectives on a Changing Scene* (Charlottesville: University of Virginia Press, 1994), 67.

8 James Clyde Mitchell, ed., *Social Networks in Urban Situations: Analysis of Personal Relationships in Central African Towns* (Manchester: Manchester University Press for Rhodes-Livingstone Institute, 1969).

9 Mayer, 'Migrancy and the Study of Africans in Towns'.

10 Melville Herskovits, 'The Negro in the New World: The Statement of a Problem', *American Anthropologist* 32, no. 1 (1930): 150.

11 Patrick Harries, 'Symbols and Sexuality: Culture and Identity on the Early Witwatersrand Gold Mines', *Gender & History* 2, no. 3 (1 September 1990): 318.

12 Arjun Appadurai, 'The Past as a Scarce Resource', *Man* 16, no. 2 (1981): 201–19.

13 Maurice Halbwachs, *On Collective Memory* (Chicago: University of Chicago Press, 1992).

14 Johannes Fabian, 'Remembering the Other: Knowledge and Recognition in the Exploration of Central Africa', *Critical Inquiry* 26, no. 1 (1999): 51.

15 David C. Berliner, 'The Abuses of Memory: Reflections on the Memory Boom in Anthropology', *Anthropological Quarterly* 78, no. 1 (2005): 198.

16 James Ferguson, *Expectations of Modernity: Myths and Meanings of Urban Life on the Zambian Copperbelt* (Berkeley: University of California Press, 1999).

17 Mayer, 'Migrancy and the Study of Africans in Towns'.

18 Mayer, 'Migrancy and the Study of Africans in Towns', 578.

18 Here, I draw on a phenomenological understanding of how we relate to the world around us and how this relationship, in turn, shapes the forms of sociality we live (see eg. Pierre Bourdieu, 'The Kabyle House or the World Reversed', in *Algeria 1960* (Cambridge: Cambridge University Press, 1979), 133–53; Richard Sennett, *The Conscience of the Eye: The Design and Social Life in Cities* (New York: Knopf, 1990); Setha M. Low, 'The Anthropology of Cities: Imagining and Theorizing the City', *Annual Review of Anthropology* 25 (1996): 383–409.)

20 Marcel Mauss, 'Les Techniques Du Corps', *Journal de Psychologie* 32, no. 3–4 (1934): 1–23; Alfred Schütz and Thomas Luckmann, *The Structures of the Life-World* (London: Heinemann, 1974).

21 Paul Connerton, *How Societies Remember* (Cambridge: Cambridge University Press, 1989), 94.

22 Connerton, *How Societies Remember*.

23 E. E. Evans-Pritchard, *Social Anthropology and Other Essays* (New York: The Free Press, 1964), 174.

24 E. E. Evans-Pritchard, 'Social Anthropology: Past and Present. The Marett Lecture', *Man* 50 (1950): 121.

25 Kirsten Hastrup, 'Introduction', in *Social Experience and Anthropological Knowledge*, ed. Kirsten Hastrup and Peter Hervik, European Association of Social Anthropologists (London: Routledge, 1994), 9.

26 Richard Werbner, 'Beyond Oblivion: Confronting Memory Crisis', in *Memory and the Postcolony: African Anthropology and the Critique of Power*, ed. Richard Werbner (London: Zed Books, 1998), 1–17.

27 Pierre Bourdieu, *Outline of a Theory of Practice*, trans. Richard Nice (Cambridge: Cambridge University Press, 1977).

28 While some anthropologists integrate the body and the senses into their phenomenological approaches to the study of the production of memory (cf. Stoller 1995), most scholars apply a Foucauldian reading of the body, which is limited to the representational, discursive level.

29 Isaac Schapera, 'The Anthropologist's Approach to Ethno-History' (presented at the Historians in Tropical Africa, Leverhulme Inter-Collegiate History Conference, University College of Rhodesia and Nyasaland, 1960), 14.

30 E. E. Evans-Pritchard, *Anthropology and History: A Lecture Delivered in the University of Manchester* (Manchester: Manchester University Press, 1961), 18.

31 Godfrey Wilson and Monica Hunter, *The Study of African Society*, The Rhodes Livingstone Papers 2 (Livingstone, Northern Rhodesia: The Rhodes Livingstone Institute, 1942), 5.

32 Marshall Sahlins, *Islands of History* (University of Chicago Press, 2013), 144.

Jürg Schneider

Photography and the Demise of Anthropology

Looking at a scholar's bibliography opens a window to his or her life, to his or her changing interests in various academic subjects over time—in short, the twists and turns of a professional academic career. Some topics come up only once and disappear without leaving any further traces. Others emerge strongly and turn into research fields on which the scholar will focus for several decades if not the rest of his or her life. Most often, such research interests run parallel to developments in the scholar's own discipline or to those in adjacent disciplines, but they may also be ahead of their time or just following a trend and a personal momentary enthusiasm. All this is certainly also true for Patrick Harries' career, which in terms of publishing spans the period from 1977 to this very day. It shows a scholar's interest in a wide range of topics (also a broad geographical interest) in African Studies, and not least, a social historian's strong propensity for anthropology.[1]

'Labour' is the first word in a paper Patrick gave in London in the late 1970s (published in 1977).[2] Patrick was then in his late 20s and teaching African History at UCT, and he would go on to engage the topic of labour migration and migrant workers in Mozambique and South Africa for twenty years without ever completely abandoning it. In the late 1990s, Patrick became increasingly interested in mechanisms of knowledge production and dissemination in and through a hermeneutic triangle formed by the sciences (to which he added anthropology), colonialism, and Christianity, in particular mission societies. Books and articles such as 'The Imperialism of Truth: Colonialism and the Natural Sciences' (1996),[3] *Butterflies and Barbarians: Swiss Missionaries and Systems of Knowledge in South-East Africa* (2007),[4] 'From the Alps to Africa: Swiss Missionaries and the Rise of Anthropology' (2007)[5] or *The Spiritual in the Secular: Missionaries and Knowledge about Africa* (2012)[6] discussed the discursive and geographical relations and mutual dependencies of the triangle's respective sides. In recent years, he has added slavery and the trans-Atlantic slave trade to his fields of research.

Although Patrick, according to my perception and reading, has never been a visual historian in the strict sense of the term, he has always been very interested in the visual, particularly photographic images, and their place in and contributions to the mechanisms of knowledge production within colonialism, anthropology and missionary endeavours in Africa. This is apparent from a number of PhD theses he supervised at the University of Basel but is also reflected in an early paper Patrick presented in 1999 at the Iziko South African Museum in Cape Town at the occasion of the conference 'Encounters with Photography: Photographing People in Southern Africa, 1860 to 1999'.

In the first part of 'Photography and the Rise of Anthropology: Henri Alexandre Junod and the Thonga of Mozambique and South Africa', Patrick looked at the way in which Swiss missionaries working in the Northern Transvaal used photographs for missionary propaganda. In the second part, he showed how anthropology, a hand-maid of colonialism and a rising academic discipline since the mid-nineteenth century, used the methodology and rhetoric of the natural sciences—one of whose tools was photography—'to provide anthropological texts with the power and authority that created a unique academic discipline'.[7]

Henri Alexandre Junod, a Francophone Swiss missionary and anthropologist working in South Africa between 1889 and 1920, was evidently not the first to recognize photography as a powerful tool in the hands of anthropologists. Leading protagonists of the emerging scientific disciplines ethnology and anthropology in nineteenth century Germany, such as Adolf Bastian or Gustav Fritsch, for instance, were much aware of photography's importance in their work.[8] The camera was understood and expected to meticulously and truthfully record what was observed and described, thus avoiding the pitfalls of subjective representation as in drawings or paintings.[9] Principles for the production of standardized and consequently comparable ethnographic and particularly anthropological photographs were made public by the Berlin based physiologist and anthropologist Gustav Fritsch, first anonymously in 1872, and three years later in Georg von Neumayer's *Anleitung zu wissenschaftlichen Beobachtungen auf Reisen*.[10] When writing about photography as a research tool Fritsch could rely on his experiences while travelling in South Africa between 1863 and 1866.[11] Neumayer's *Anleitung* was published at almost the same time as 'Notes and Queries on Anthropology'[12] in Britain and it was also during this period that the first anthropological photo albums were compiled and published.

In fact, Patrick had already written a short article about Henri Alexandre Junod in 1981. But now, in 1999 and roughly two decades later, he combined his accumulated research interests and the imperially and globally working knowledge systems—the natural sciences, anthropology, mission societies and, to a lesser extent, the colonial state—in one essay. Evidently, both Patrick and the conveners were in sync with their time and (what W. J. T. Mitchell and Gottfried Boehm had been propagating as) the "iconic" or "pictorial turn". Photographs were finally regarded as powerful resources and not mere illustrations for academic research and, since the early 1980s, had been gradually establishing themselves as a distinguished archival category. Vera Viditz-Ward's work on photography and African photographers, which appeared in the mid-1980s, reverberated strongly to historians' and anthropologists' research work and triggered an ongoing stream of research on African photographers. Christraud Geary and Paul Jenkins began to work on photography in Africa; Jenkins, in particular worked on mission photography that in turn was the starting point for the digitization of the Basel Mission's photo archive.[13] Thomas Theye's *Der geraubte Schatten* appeared in 1989.[14] Another major contribution to the expanding field of visual studies was *Anthropology and Photography*[15] edited by Elizabeth Edwards in 1992, which lent its

Hunters hunted. Coverage of the Minister of Communication's visit to the Buea Press Photo Archives. Buea, Cameroon, April 2013. Picture: Rosario Mazuela.

title to the RAI conference in London in May 2014, indeed the very brainchild of this early key work. Furthermore, in the very year of the Cape Town conference in 1999 at the Iziko South African Museum, Wolfram Hartmann, Jeremy Silvester and Patricia Hayes published *The Colonising Camera*, convincingly linking Namibia's colonial past and the use of the camera and photographic images in the process of colonisation.[16] In fact, many of the early protagonists of the "iconic turn" in African and Visual Studies—Elizabeth Edwards, Christraud Geary, Patricia Hayes, Chris Morton, to name but a few—participated in the Cape Town conference.

Most evidently, as the RAI conference in London convincingly showed, photography has not led to the demise of anthropology. The title of this short essay, however, is more than just a catchy phrase as it points to the dynamic, changing and still developing relationship between the two. Indeed, the initial phase of euphoria, when the emerging discipline enthusiastically embraced photography as the ideal and timely tool for research and documentation, soon gave way to a more sober atmosphere and subsequently a rather strained relationship with its visual past.[17] At the same time,

African photographer at work at the station of Oyem, at the occasion of Mr and Mrs Beigbeder's visit.
Picture: Anita Gay, Oyem, Gabon, ca. 1950–1965 (copyright Défap-Service protestant de mission,
reference number GA.PP.068-04104).

anthropology took up the challenge of reflecting its own history and practices. Through *Expanding the Frame*,[18] a great number of photographs have travelled back to the places where they were taken in the nineteenth century, triggering necessary and long due conversations between anthropologists and the local communities as well as among members of those communities. Indeed, Edwards and Morton observe 'an enormous expansion in recent years of interest in, and analytical attention to, the historical relationship between anthropology and photography [which] is sustained by a body of critical writing on visual matters over several decades'.[19] We are proud to say that Patrick was one of those scholars who has from an early stage onwards contributed to this body of critical writing.

1   This is most apparent in Patrick's farewell lecture in Basel entitled 'History and Anthropology: A Dance to the Music of Time', 11 December 2014.

2   Patrick Harries, 'Labour Migration from the Delagoa Bay Hinterland to South Africa, 1858–1896' in *Institute of Commonwealth Studies* (London, Collected Seminar Papers, 1977).

3   Patrick Harries, 'The Imperialism of Truth: Colonialism and the Natural Sciences' (Collected Seminar Papers of the Basler Afrika Bibliographien, Basel, Switzerland, 1996).

4   Patrick Harries, *Butterflies and Barbarians: Swiss Missionaries and Systems of Knowledge in South-East Africa* (Ohio: Ohio University Press, 2007).

5   Patrick Harries, 'From the Alps to Africa: Swiss Missionaries and the Rise of Anthropology' in eds. Helen Tilley Robert J. Gordon, *Ordering Africa. Anthropology, European Imperialism and the Politics of Knowledge* (Manchester: Manchester University Press, 2007), 201–224.

6   Patrick Harries and David Maxwell, eds., *The Spiritual in the Secular: Missionaries and Knowledge about Africa* (Grand Rapids, MI: Wm. B. Eerdmans Publishing, 2012).

7   Patrick Harries, 'Photography and the Rise of Anthropology: Henri-Alexandre Junod and the Thonga of Mozambique and South Africa', in *Encounters with Photography: Photographing People in Southern Africa, 1860–1999*, Proceedings of the Conference held at the South African Museum, Cape Town, 1999 (Rondebosch, South Africa: University of Cape Town Press, 2000).

8   Jürg Schneider, 'Vom formulierten Anspruch zur kontrollierten Produktion. Das Ringen der frühen deutschen Ethnologie und Anthropologie um Standardisierung und Vergleichbarkeit fotografischer Aufnahmen', *Baessler-Archiv*, N. F. 57 (2009): 59–73.

9   Hartmut Krech, *Ein Bild der Welt. Voraussetzungen der anthropologischen Fotografie* (Konstanz: Hartung-Gorre Verlag, 1989).

10   Anonymous [Fritsch, Gustav], 'I. Photographie', in *Rathschläge für anthropologische Untersuchungen auf Expeditionen der Marine. Auf Veranlassung des Chefs der Kaiserlich Deutschen Admiralität ausgearbeitet von der Berliner Gesellschaft für Anthropologie, Ethnologie und Urgeschichte, Zeitschrift für Ethnologie*, vol. 4., Berlin (1872): 325–356. Gustav Fritsch, 'Praktische Gesichtspunkte zur Verwendung zweier dem Reisenden wichtigen technischen Hilfsmittel: Das Mikroskop und der photographische Apparat,' in *Anleitung zu wissenschaftlichen Beobachtungen auf Reisen in Einzel-Abhandlungen*, ed. Georg von Neumayer, 2 vols, third edition, (Hannover: Dr. Max Jänecke, Verlagsbuchhandlung, 1906): 731–814.

11   Gustav Fritsch, *Die Eingeborenen Süd-Afrika's* (Breslau: Hirt, 1872).

12   James Urry, '"Notes and Queries on Anthropology" and the Development of Field Methods in British Anthropology, 1870–1920', *Proceedings of the Royal Anthropological Institute of Great Britain and Ireland* 1972 (1972): 45–57.

13   Basel Mission Image Archive http://bmpix.usc.edu/bmpix/controller/index.htm accessed 24 November 2014.

14   Thomas Theye, ed., *Der geraubte Schatten: Die Photographie als ethnographisches Dokument* (München: Münchner Stadtmuseum, 1989).

15   Elizabeth Edwards, ed., *Anthropology and Photography* (New Haven: Yale University Press, 1992).

16   Wolfram Hartmann, Jeremy Silvester, and Patricia Hayes, *The Colonising Camera: Photographs in the Making of Namibian History* (Cape Town: University of Cape Town Press, 1999).

17   Elizabeth Edwards, 'Setting the Focus', in *Made to be Seen. Perspectives on the History of Visual Anthropology*, eds. Marcus Banks and Jay Ruby (Chicago and London: The University of Chicago Press, 2011): 159–189.

18   Elizabeth Edwards and Christopher Morton, *Photography, Anthropology and History: Expanding the Frame* (Farnham, Surrey UK: Ashgate Publishing, 2012).

19   Edwards and Morton, *Photography, Anthropology and History*, 2.

Gregor Dobler

Staying for Gold or Joining the Rebellion?
South West African Migrant Workers on the Rand
During War and Genocide, 1904–1905

Migratory labour is one of the most significant forces in twentieth century Southern African history. In Namibian historiography, it has mostly been seen as a disruptive force. The migratory labour system split the country into core and peripheral zones and set rural economies on the path to dependency. It facilitated economic integration while making continued separation of "black" and "white" living spheres conceivable, making apartheid policies appear necessary and possible to the white minority. Seen in the light of a system that developed fully after World War II, it is difficult to understand why people from rural northern Namibia started to look for employment in the first place. Nationalist historiography in Namibia and beyond has often sought to explain this conundrum with colonial violence, extraction and dispossession or, slightly later, with the greed of local chiefs and kings who sent young men for work in order to profit from their wages.

From the 1970s, a new generation of historians, Patrick Harries among them, challenged this view by stressing that early migrants often looked for work out of their own will and pursued their own aims. A system of injustice and dependency was the outcome of the process, not its initial driving force. As I have argued elsewhere[1], early labour migration from northern Namibia can illustrate this point. Young men went to work long before colonial domination could force them to do so. They looked for new ways of social ascent within their society. Tapping external resources through the sale of their labour was, for them, a way of empowerment. This made it difficult to perceive that their emancipatory actions cumulated to integrate their society into a system of exploitation.

In the very early years of migratory labour, however, before a contract system had been institutionalised in South West Africa, several hundred workers were forced to experience the systemic character of migrant labour and its connections to colonial domination. During the colonial war and genocide in 1904, almost a thousand South West Africans were working in gold mines on the Witwatersrand. A sporadic and unreliable stream of news reached them from home and confronted them with a difficult decision: should they stay and fulfil their contract, or should they leave and join the fight of their people? In this paper, I will show how the systemic link between migratory labour and colonial domination became very visible to them, while the separation of colonial powers prevented them from systematically criticising migratory labour.

Telling their story requires some context. Why did South West Africans work on the Rand mines in the first place? Indentured workers from South West Africa had worked in the Cape Colony during the 1870s and 1880s[2], but after 1884, labour needs in the new colony started to grow. Big infrastructure projects around the turn of the century (railway lines and the Swakopmund harbour), the industrialisation of copper mining, the discovery of diamonds in 1908 and the influx of settlers after the war made South West African labour needs more difficult to fulfil—all the more so after most central Namibian workers had been killed, displaced or alienated in the war and genocide. For a long time, the authorities anxiously tried to keep "their" workers in the colony.

In 1902, however, the situation still seemed fairly stable, and the newly established Witwatersrand Native Labour Association (WNLA), which was in constant need for additional workers, gained permission to recruit in German South West Africa.[3] Of each worker, WNLA had to pay 20 Marks to the German government. Contracts were formed for two years, and the employer had to take charge of the workers' transport back to Swakopmund. The employer had to deposit 200 Marks with the German authorities as security for the migrants' return; this money was deducted from the workers' wages and only paid after they had fulfilled the contract and returned to Namibia.[4] 625 recruits were shipped from Swakopmund to Cape Town in 1903 and transported by rail to the Rand. When the war broke out in January 1904, recruiting was cut short, but 282 Herero who had lived in the vicinity of Swakopmund and had been taken prisoner were 'recruited' by the WNLA, as well.[5] For the next two years, the workers lived and worked in exile while the German authorities committed atrocities on their friends and relatives at home. For Herero oral historians, labour recruitment appears in retrospect as one of the major reasons for the war.[6] A missionary source that so far seems to have been overlooked by Namibianists sheds light on a different link between the uprising and migrant labour: the exile community on the Rand closely followed the events and was thereby confronted with difficult decisions.

Friedrich Bernsmann is a well-known figure in Namibian history. Born in Barmen in 1845, he was sent to Namibia by the Rhenish Missionary Society RMG in 1873. He worked as a missionary in Otjimbingue and Omburo and remained in the country until his death in 1920. In 1904, the war made it impossible for him to continue his missionary work. He took leave to live with his daughters in Johannesburg and Pretoria, and he used the occasion to visit the South West African workers on the Rand mines almost weekly between October 1904 and April 1905, and three more times in May, July and August 1905. His letters about the visits have been conserved in the VEM archives in Wuppertal (RMG 1613d). The letters to the Mission Head Office from South Africa were dated 21 December 1904 (L1), 10 March 1905 (L2), 27 April 1905 (L3), 19 July 1905 (L4). A further letter dated 10 July 1905, was sent to the German colonial government in Windhoek (L5). After his return to Karibib, Bernsmann sent two final letters about his experiences in South Africa on 2 October 1905 (L6) and 28 October 1905 (L7).

According to Bernsmann (L1), South West Africans worked in six mines: Lancaster, Lancaster West (together 404 South West Africans; in Lancaster West mostly

worked 'Herero who had been brought to Swakopmund in the beginning of the re-
bellion and had let themselves be contracted for the mines'), Crown Deep (125
Herero), Fereira Deep (25 Herero, 49 Ovambo), Nourse Deep (22 Herero, 48
Ovambo) and Geldenhuis Deep (48 Ovambo). He also mentions one Damara and five
Nama speakers among the Christians who attended his services. Of the 910 South
West African workers who, according to Bernsmann, had reached the mines, at least
100 (probably more) had already 'deserted' by mid-1904. Another 89 had died in the
first year of their contract, according to figures given by the workers and confirmed
by the mine managements. The mortality rate of more than 10% (12.65% for Oshi-
vambo and 11.34% for Otjiherero speakers) was extreme even for the gold mines. Most
deaths seem to have been caused by pneumonia.

There were many reasons to leave the contract, even though it implied losing a
substantial part of one's wages. Labour conditions were hard, but they seem to have
been accepted as a matter of course. Miners worked six days a week in twelve-hour
shifts lasting from six to six; they changed weekly from day to night shifts. Mine su-
perintendents generally considered the South West Africans to be very good workers,
especially those who had already worked on the railway construction sites.

Housing does not seem to have been a reason for complaint. Workers lived in the
usual compounds, subdivided in rooms of 4 to 5 by 8 to 10 metres. In each room, a
double row of wooden boards 'which look like shelves for trade goods' (L1) and were
devoid of matresses provided sleeping room for thirty people. In Fereira Deep, the
mine's Herero shared one room; the neighbouring room was occupied by Ovambo
workers.

Food was more of a problem. South West Africans did not like the porridge made
from coarse maize meal which was served as staple food on the mines, and which workers from Bechuanaland and South Africa gave some taste with sugar or spices; the
Herero instead asked (unsuccessfully) for porridge made from wheat (L1, L2). The most
vivid complaint about labour conditions was about individual cruelty of white super-
visors. The number of desertions on the Lancaster mines strongly decreased when, after
many complaints, management replaced a particularly detested supervisor (L1, L5).

The main motivation to go to work on the mines and to endure the hardships
was clearly money. Workers seem not to have questioned the level of wages, but they
felt cheated because Sundays were not included in the duration of the contract. A pay-
ticket (which they had taken to be for the month of 30 days) was issued every 30
working days only, so that 20 tickets covered 24 months. According to Philippus Hans,
a Christian miner whom Bernsmann had known from Omburo, miners spent their
wages on clothing, luggage, 'unnecessary things', in particular on good food, and 'some
Ovambo on Fereira Deep even with black whores' (L3). The Christians among them
were enthusiastic about books, as well, and asked Bernsmann to obtain (Christian)
books for them for which they willingly paid. Some who had wanted to have their
wives come from South West Africa to live with them had not been able to save
enough money to do so (L1).

These few details in Bernsmann's letters about life on the mines do not stand out as unusual. What makes the letters unique is his account of Herero miners' relation to the war at home. From their first meeting, South West Africans, particularly the Otji-herero speakers, showed a passionate interest in hearing Bernsmann's accounts of the events. The miners were already well informed about the general situation. A number of them had been in the country when the uprising started, and when 'rumours' about the war reached them, 80–90 Herero had left Lancaster and Crown Deep mines and reached the uprising through the Kalahari by March or April 1904. Their colleagues in the mines, in turn, had been informed of this by a letter Asser Mutjinde, a former mission teacher and scribe to the Chiefs of Omaruru, had written from Walvis Bay.

Bernsmann, even though biased, was a welcome first-hand witness. On 6 November 1904, he told miners at Lancaster Mine

> about the revolt of their compatriots and what I had experienced, also how other missionaries had fared in it; I told them of the great suffering the revolt had caused us, and how we had to grieve for our lost parishes and their entire people, who had not wanted to listen to our admonitions and warnings and were now come to distress and perdition. I added a few admonitions, especially that they should now work quietly and diligently and follow their supervisors until they had served their time. Those who might be tempted to run to their fellow countrymen would only fall into the same distress and perdition.

He later held a service and preached from Mark 12:17: 'Render to Ceasar the things that are Ceasar's and to God the things that are God's'. 'They listened', Bernsmann wrote, 'to my news and admonitions in deep and solemn silence. Some seemed ill pleased; they got up and left' (L1). Despite the admonitions, and to his embarrassment, twelve more Herero deserted the next day. To exculpate himself, Bernsmann linked their departure to cruelty on the mine, but his account might at least have played a triggering role. At later visits, he notes, 'I had a smaller audience at the services on the mines. Perhaps it would have been smaller still if the demand for news from home had not driven some to attend. I conveyed those, of course, in a gentle manner, since they mostly contained defeats, bondage, hunger and affliction of their people. What they thought about the news, they did not tell me. They listened with gravity and in silence' (L1).

Miners obviously compared his report with news that had reached them from home. Bernsmann was asked to read out the fragment of a letter by Asser Mutjinde to the miners. The long letter of at least twenty pages had obviously been copied and shared; Bernsmann saw one fragment at Nourse Deep, another one at Fereira Deep. The fragment, written before the disastrous battle at Waterberg, revealed that the people from Omaruru had started the rebellion because the Germans had wanted to kill Chief Michael and his headmen, and gave an account of the heroic and glorious fights of the Herero against the usurpers.

Gerhard Afrika, who together with Asser had been dispatched by Michael Tjisiseta to Walvis Bay with nineteen men to buy arms, and was apprehended there by the British, also had written a letter to the miners. He obviously knew many of them by name and instructed them to contribute to the struggle by giving donations to Gerhard and Asser— in Bernsmann's words: 'You, N, will give £1.10.-, you, X, will give £1.10.- etc.'. This speaks for a well-established contact between exiles and those in the country. Philippus Hans indeed entrusted £6.10.- to Bernsmann together with a letter to Asser. Bernsmann sent them to missionary Böhm in Walvis Bay. Since Asser had gone to the Nababeb Copper Mines in Namaqualand, the money was finally handed to Gerhard Afrika.

Not only Herero remained in contact with their families. On 27 November 1904, Oshivambo-speaking miners from Fereira Deep gave Bernsmann 50 letters to friends and relatives, which he sent to the Finnish Missionaries Rautanen and Pettinen in Ovamboland to be delivered (L1, L3).

The news from home that reached the miners through this network of information generated hot and continuing debates. Two questions were crucial: should they even remain in South Africa until the end of their contracts? If so, would they be able to re-turn home via Swakopmund, which would hand them into the power of the Germans?

As we have seen, many opted to return to South West Africa. By mid-1905, only 617 South West African workers were left in the Rand mines; many had died, but more than 200, most of them Herero, seem to have left their contracts. 'One told me', Bernsmann writes, 'that, if they had to die, it was better to flee and die in their own country' (L5).

The remaining workers approached the end of their contracts. Could they rely on the Germans to let them join their surviving families after collecting the money due to them in Swakopmund? For Oshivambo-speaking workers, this does not seem to have been a problem; they were keen on returning through Swakopmund and join-ing their families. For Herero, the decision was much more difficult. They asked Bernsmann, who inquired with the authorities and received the information from the new German consul in South Africa, Foretsch, that 'in fact those Herero who should return to their country would have to be subject to a certain supervision (*unter einer gewissen Aufsicht gehalten werden müssten*)', so that it might be better for them to stay another year on contract in South Africa (L6). If they did not return via Swakopmund, the salary withheld would be paid out to their relatives held in custody.

When Bernsmann left South Africa in late August 1905, few Herero workers were tempted to return via Swakopmund. Most were determined either to stay under British authority or to take the long and insecure road through the Kalahari in a wagon, to join the remaining Herero in Bechuanaland or reach their homes without meeting the *Ovan-deutsa*. As Bernsmann's godchild Ernst Heinrich Kamekaunda wrote to him from Lan-caster on 18 August 1905:

> We will surely not go by the sea, but remain with the [British] Government. As regards
> the money of which you are writing that we should go and receive it in Windhuk, we

will surely not do so. It is arranged for us to be a snare to us, for us to go to our death. We are forced to give up the money; we do not really care, but will seek to gain more.—If God lets you reach our country safely, let us know everything you hear from our world; we will answer immediately. (L7)

Friedrich Bernsmann's letters give us a glimpse into the anxieties and predicament of miners trapped in a double dilemma. They felt with their relatives and friends at home and would have liked to join them, but could only do so by breaking contract, forfeiting a good part of their earning and risking death. Their pay was withheld by the very German authorities who had become their enemies. For the first time, contract labour and colonial domination appeared as closely interlinked factors of injustice. Why, then, did people continue to work for the colonial economy as contract workers after the immediate crisis ended? Many factors contributed, of course, and they have been amply treated in the literature—from economic crisis to the wish for individual advancement and the absence of sufficiently lucrative alternatives. Bernsmann's accounts highlight a further factor: in the experience of South West African miners in South Africa, the systematic linkage between colonial authority and the contract system was broken by the difference in authorities. The mines themselves were under British control, and staying with 'the government' offered shelter from the Germans. Even though the miners witnessed the most cruel form of colonial domination at the same time as the downsides of the contract labour system, they experienced the mines as distinct from the German authorities. As Ernst Kamekaunda continued his letter: 'God's words are dear to our hearts, but we very much fear the evil ways of the Germans. We will remain with the English' (L7). Ten years later, 'the English' took over colonial rule in South West Africa. The comparative colonial experience of the South West African exile community on the Rand might have had crucial influence on the attitude towards the new colonial masters and made local society more willing to accept the continuing institutionalisation of the migrant labour system.

1   Gregor Dobler, *Traders and Trade in Colonial Ovambo-land, 1925–1990* (Basel: Basler Africa Bibliographien, 2014).
2   See Jan-Bart Gewald, 'Untapped Sources: Slave Exports from Southern and Central Namibia up to the Mid-Nineteenth Century', in *The Mfecane Aftermath*, ed. C. Hamilton (Johannesburg: University of the Witwatersrand Press, 1995), 417-435; and Dag Henrichsen, 'Damara Labour Recruitment to the Cape Colony and Marginalisation and Hegemony in late 19th century Central Namibia', *Journal of Namibian Studies* 3 (2008): 63–82.
3   For the most complete account so far, see Jan-Bart Gewald, 'The Road of the Man Called Love and the Sack of Sero: The Herero-German War and the Export of Herero Labour to the South African Rand', *Journal of African History* 40, no. 1 (1999): 21–40.
4   *Südafrikanische Wochenschrift*, 28.11.1902, 170.
5   Gewald, 'The Road', 26f.
6   Gewald, 'The Road'.

Cassandra Mark-Thiesen

From Mining Pit to Missionary Bungalow:
Trading Spaces in the Writing of Patrick Harries

Location! Location! Location!

In many respects, when a historian commits to a specific research topic he or she is also committing to a predetermined space of potential travel and scholarly engagement. The decision to follow a particular intellectual interest demands visits to certain archives and conferences, as well as intense engagement with a more or less set selection of scholars. This network, the historian's home, is a keystone of academic achievement, wealth (in knowledge, of course!), and emotional stability. But as hinted in the previous sentence, the scholar's geographical space is not all that becomes shaped by these choices. Regularly taken for granted is the transformation of the researcher's "headspace", or mental space, as he or she attempts to reconstruct a time and place for things worth learning. Indeed, the emotional landscape surrounding particular historical real estate may occasionally (perhaps subconsciously) drive historians to choose more cleverly in the future.

Throughout his scholarly career Patrick Harries has made a noticeable transition from the deep, dark, depressive underworld of late nineteenth and early twentieth century South African mines to the top of the hill—the easy, breezy life at contemporary Swiss mission stations in South East Africa. Without proposing any straightforward causal relation, this essay revisits the mining world that consumed Patrick during the composition of his PhD dissertation, and which came to life for a wider audience in his celebrated book *Work, Culture, and Identity: Migrant Labourers in Mozambique and South Africa, C. 1860–1910* (1994), to make the point that ... well, if there was a bit causality, who could blame him?

Patrick's first book was enthusiastically welcomed and widely celebrated, 'not simply as a piece of labour history but as a major contribution to our understanding of the modern evolution of southern Africa.'[1] His was a 'path-breaking' historical study, according to his peers.[2] Leroy Vail, the too soon departed professor of African history at Harvard University, announced that 'there is a major new voice to be heard in Southern African studies'. *Work, Culture, and Identity* told the story of Mozambican migrant labourers working on plantations, diamond fields, and gold mines in South Africa between 1860 and 1910. Though touching on a variety of their workplaces, the book has retained a reputation as one pertaining to mining history, imagery from the Kimberly mines especially having left a lasting impression in the minds of its readers.

The mine's subterranean structures carried an air of both fascination and fear. Objectively speaking, underground mining was a technical revelation of this period. Patrick envisioned the underground works of the Kimberly and De Beers mines as 'a honey comb of tunnels beneath'.[3] Yet, there was little sweet or tender about this triumph of technology. Instead,

> [l]ong tunnels were driven off the shaft, at intervals of forty feet, through the hard rock at the edge of the mine. From these tunnels a large number of small, timbered galleries were dug through the diamondiferous blue ground to the opposite wall of the mine, where they were widened into stopes. Once these neighbouring galleries were joined, they formed chambers often as large as 100 feet long, 20 feet wide, and 20 feet high.[4]

Human excavation with the help of drills and dynamite had carved out an anthill-like infrastructure that reached over 400 meters below ground.[5] Optically speaking, underground mining had few redeeming qualities.

Both mechanised diamond and gold mining played an important part in the economic development of the early South African Republic. Moreover, both industries seemed to be undergoing similar advances around the turn of the century. Indeed my own research on gold mining in Ghana between 1877 and 1910 shows numerous similarities in appearance between the underworlds that came to shape in these regions. A deep fascination with what lay underneath was certainly recorded in the travel diaries of Lady Decima Guggisberg and her husband the colonial administrator and British military officer Frederick Gordon Guggisberg when they visited one of the Gold Coast's most productive gold mining concessions in 1905. The Abbontiakoon Mine atmosphere 'damp, warm and oppressive in spite of the air that was continually being forced through the levels by the pumping engines, felt curious and unnatural.'[6] Hearing senses peaked: 'Every now and then a rattling sound would come from behind us, there would be shouts to "stand clear," and we would press close to the rocky wall while a truck laden with ore would clatter past amid a chorus of cries and yells from the natives working near us [...]'.[7] At times the visuals were breathtaking:

> I was surrounded by gold, walking on it, touching it with my hands, sometimes accidentally and painfully ramming my helmet into it. It was not pure gold, of course, nor could one see it, but it was there, mixed up with the rock, being hewn out with drills and dynamite, rattling past me in the trucks—the gold that makes the world go round, I was fairly in it.[8]

Nevertheless, a looming sense of horror remained. In attempting to relay this feeling back to their white audience, the authors projected upon the bodies of the black miners they had encountered that day during their tour. They write,

The scene in these deep "levels" was strange and bewildering. The natives, naked but for a loin cloth, looked in the gloomy galleries like huge black demons as they toiled and sweated with pick and shovel at the ore around them, a faint flicker of light from the candles flashing occasionally from their white eyeballs, or shining from their white teeth. Indeed, I would often have stumbled headlong into a man if it had not been for those white teeth, gleaming like danger signals in the darkness. [9]

The fears of these visitors, however, did not bear comparison with the nightmarish scenarios that the miners themselves were confronted with on a daily basis.

Before the 1880s and 1890s, before the dawn of professional deep shaft mining, flooded and collapsed levels and shafts were a real and constant threat. Harries noted that

By the end of 1873 the open cast Kimberly mine had reached a depth of almost 200 feet and was experiencing problems as the surrounding shale slid into the mine and covered the claims with debris. Work was further restricted when summer rainfall turned the pit floor into quagmire and flooded the deeper claims. Workers lived in fear of someone tapping a "greasy slide" at its base and in this way causing a great block of earth to slither into the pit, and, after the great "reef" fall in November 1873, they lived under the shadow of a lengthening wall that threatened to collapse on them. [10]

A most striking description of this terror could not be contained even by his sober writing. As Patrick points out in the book, underground mining revolutionised the labour process by bringing skills and higher pay to local mineworkers. [11] Nevertheless, for all of its great potential and magnificence, it is difficult to ignore the uglier side of the early beginnings of deep level mining in Africa; the frequency of potential death and destruction constantly weighing heavily on the historian's mind.

Location! Location! Re-Location?

It is difficult to ignore contrast between aforementioned mining space and the spatial setting of Patrick's later research. Compare these underground structures to the hilltop edifices located on sprawling estates that stood tall in *Butterflies and Barbarians*. Zen philosophy emphasizes that the space we live in can have a therapeutic effect on ourselves that it is important to think wisely about the spaces in which we spend our days and nights. Arguably, this concept is not entirely lost on scholars either. The emotional texture that inhabits historians with each new project cannot be wished away. Indeed it is part of the procedure of historical investigation. And though neither ensuring a good mental nor geographical space should be at the top of one's mind when finalizing research projects, perhaps it ought not to be entirely ignored either. Luckily, every few years an opportunity for relocation arises.

1   Roy Bridges, review of *Work, Culture, Identity: Migrant Laborers in Mozambique and South Africa, c.1860–1910*, by Patrick Harries, *History*, 84, no. 275 (1999): 481.

2   Kathleen Sheldon, review of *Work, Culture, Identity*, by Patrick Harries, *African Studies Review*, 38, no. 02 (1995): 158–160.

3   Patrick Harries, *Work, Culture, and Identity: Migrant Laborers in Mozambique and South Africa, c. 1860–1910* (London: Heinemann, 1994), 69.

4   Ibid.

5   Ibid.

6   Decima Moore Guggisberg and Frederick G. Guggisberg, *We Two in West Africa* (New York: Charles Scribner's Sons, 1909), 137.

7   Ibid.

8   Ibid.

9   Ibid.

10 Patrick Harries, *Work, Culture, and Identity*, 48.

11 Ibid., 69.

Ulrike Sill

Of Wives, Slaves and Commerce, or:
The Price of Things

What is the value of a human being? What would be, let us say, the cost of a concubine? How expensive is life in a far away place? What goods will be available? And how does one pay for them? A document in the archives of the Basel Mission dating from 1859 gives insight into the market situation in the West African trading fort of Christiansborg/Osu (now part of the Ghanaian capital Accra) and the neighbouring coastal region.

In the year 1859 the Basel missionary Carl Aldinger was about to take on a new appointment within the mission field on the Gold Coast but was duty-bound to send a quarterly report to the mission's board in Basel.[1] This may have been the reason why he chose a general topic: 'The Circulation of Money on the Gold Coast—Past and Present'. The document oscillates between abolitionism agitprop on the one hand and, on the other hand, basic information one might expect from a guidebook today. It also reflects the local and the long-distance trading relations shaping the market in Christiansborg and its region at the time—and the different notions involved. Among these the notion of wealth was important well into the twentieth century.[2] Thus, while the slave trade on the coast no longer played a major economic role, so-called domestic slavery, as well as the institution of pawning people were much more persistent.[3] The Basel Mission was one actor, who—even before domestic slavery became illegal in 1874 under British colonial rule—had abolished domestic slavery in its congregations in 1861 and attempted to substitute "unfree labour" with "wage labour". This "slave emancipation" of 1861 not only led to serious conflict within the Basel Mission congregations and the communities in which they were situated, but opinions among the European personnel on the issue were also divided. However, a consensus on the rejection of the slave-trade prevailed in the Basel Mission.

Slaves had been a major factor in the transantlantic trade on the Gold Coast until the early nineteenth century. Aldinger infers that the trade had not yet completely stopped in 1859: 'Throughout the last weeks in Christiansborg one could watch, how whole groups of children aged 10–15 years, boys and girls, were herded towards Accra in order to be sold there. The price for a handsomely-grown, healthy youth is 50 Dollars'. Yet other, 'legitimate' trade was gradually to replace it. At the time this trade consisted mainly in palm oil. Aldinger identifies one major challenge resulting from the abolition of slavery in that in the absence of an actual currency human beings had for a long time been a means of circulation, whereas labour had no market value. Aldinger reflects on this issue in its historical dimension:

> At first one sought to address the lack of a suitable means of circulation [currency]
> through various smaller items of trade—circulating according to a certain market value.
> But because of their perishable nature, these items could not suffice. Then the cowrie
> shell offered itself as the hitherto missing means of circulation. As soon as [the shells]
> circulated, trade—especially the trade with palm oil—started to flourish.

Aldinger's association of paid labour with the promotion of commerce, as well as the
equation of this with the growth of general wealth reflects notions of the abolitionist
discourse. In this context unfree labour was perceived to be—in the long run—more
expensive than wage labour and detrimental for economic progress. It appears that
for Aldinger one key factor in the situation on the Gold Coast was the availability of
a currency—a condition sine qua non for paid labour. Cowrie shells had been imported
to Christiansborg since the early eighteenth or late seventeenth century.[4]

Aldinger provides details on the means of payment current in 1859. Especially
with regard to this he appears to make use of information gathered locally—probably
via the Basel Mission trading post established in 1854 from fellow European missionaries and local middlepersons. While his report has a political stance and objective it
also contains a wealth of information that reflects the need for Europeans and Ghana-
ians to deal with a complex system of various currencies. He mentions four different
types of currencies relevant in the Christiansborg area: (1) certain goods assuming an
additional role as currency in the past, (2) the cowrie shell, (3) various coins from across
the atlantic—either from Europe or from the Americas,[5] and, finally, (4) gold dust as
the currency of trading partners from the Asante empire and from the Akyem states
in the interior: 'In Akyem and Asante the sale [of cowrie shells] is prohibited up to
this day. In both kingdoms only gold dust is current'.[6] This situation, of course, had
implications for people crossing the border: 'Since in Akyem and Asante the Sansibarese
shells [i.e. cowries] are not yet current, any one travelling to these kingdoms either
has to equip himself with gold dust or he has to exchange his cowries for gold dust in
the last farming village of Akuapem, Hawanti'.[7]

In a situation where—because of trade—more than one currency plays a role, exchange rates are of vital interest. Aldinger not only indicates the current exchange
rates of 1859 relevant for inland trade, but also for trade across the Atlantic. He presents foreign exchange rates for cowrie shells and (American) dollars as well as for
shilling and pence, thus also providing a reference to the British currency: '1 Dollar =
80 strings. ½ Dollar = 40 strings. 1 Shilling = 16 strings. 6 Pence = 8 strings[8].' Christiansborg, like all Danish settlements, was sold to the British in 1850 but the poll tax
introduced in 1852 was to be collected partly in cowries.[9] The exchange rates appear
to have varied locally: 'In Akuapem, and especially in Krobo, where huge masses of
cowries lie buried in the ground, the Dollar is being exchanged for 85 and, at times,
for 90 strings.'

The next larger unit after the 'string' (40 cowries) was the 'head' (Ga: 'yi', or
'cabes' from the Portugese 'cabeça'[10]), which consisted of 50 strings. Aldinger explains

that 15 heads are equivalent to one load of approximately 68 lbs or one bag (Ga: 'floto'). At the time cowries appear to have been the local currency of choice, which presented the Basel Mission (and others) with rather mundane issues: 'When constructing our premises, or during other, large ventures involving a greater workforce, we have to employ one additional man to count the cowries—if not every day, then at least every Saturday'.[11] The large quantity of cowries needed in business transactions, then leads to questions about the price of things, and Aldinger provides quite a detailed list.

Aldinger records a price-list for food items as well as the price for a slave, which—as mentioned above—was 50 Dollars. The price indicated for food items give insight into the actual purchasing power of the sum mentioned. The list also documents what was literally available on the market on the coast. To give a few examples from this list:

Food item	Cost in cowries	Cost in foreign currency
1 oxen	25 heads	16 (?) Dollars
1 horse	112 heads	70 Dollars
1 sheep	3–4 ½ heads	2–3 Dollars
1 goat	1 ½–4 ½ heads	1–3 Dollars
1 chicken	15 strings	
(...)		
1 lb fish	3–6 strings	6–12 Kreuzer
1 lb dried fish	9–18 strings	18–36 Kreuzer
1 load corn (maize)		
of approximately 75 lb	1 head 30 strings	1 Dollar
1 lb maize-flour	1 string	2 Kreuzer
1 lb maize-bread	1 string	2 Kreuzer
1 lb beans	4 strings	8 Kreuzer
1 lb groundnuts	6 strings	12 Kreuzer
(...)		
1 lb soap		
(made from plantain skin)	6 strings	12 Kreuzer
1 measure of beer		
('pito' made from maize)	4 strings	8 Kreuzer
1 measure of palm wine	4 strings	8 Kreuzer
1 measure of onions	1 head	1 fl. 40 Kreuzer[12]
1 measure of red pepper	12 strings	24 Kreuzer
(...)		

Aldinger further lists the price of beef, game, pork, yam, plantains, cassava, bananas, oranges, lemons, pineapples, fire wood and other items of daily consumption.

'Counting Cowries'. Picture taken in Christiansborg by Christoph Wilhelm Locher in the early 1860s. ABM, QD-30.011.0068.

Carl Aldinger took a clear stance in opposing what he understood as slavery. He had arrived on the Gold Coast in 1858 and at the time of writing his report was almost fresh from the Basel Mission House and its training. The situation on the Gold Coast including local concepts and notions must still have been foreign to him. On the one hand, this appears to have led him to write about aspects of everyday life, which for the "old hands" were not worth mentioning. On the other hand, it made him a keen observer of anything that potentially reeked of human beings as commodity. In his case this included not only slavery, but also the practice Europeans usually called concubinage. Since the practice involved money Aldinger apparently considered it as equivalent to slavery. In one case he mentions that 28 Dollars had been 'invested' by a European '... publicly buying a Euro-African girl in order to satisfy his carnal lust for eight weeks and to dismiss her thereafter ...'. This in fact refers to a major scandal within the Basel Mission community at the time: Wilhelmine Wulff, a young Euro-African teacher at the local Basel Mission's girls' boarding school, had entered into a relationship with the commanding officer of Christiansborg.[13] At the beginning of negotiations Wilhelmine's mother, Sara Wulff, involved the Basel missionary Locher in the hope of securing a Christian marriage service. But the British officer declared that he would enter such a relationship only according to local custom. Other than what Aldinger suggests, though, the arrangement appears to be in tune with local legal standards prevailing at the time. The family of Wilhelmine Wulff had been asked and had given its consent.

48

The European staff of the Basel Mission shared the opinion that the bond between two Christians had to be solemnized in church. To resort to "local custom" without a church wedding was considered unacceptable. But—as opposed to Aldinger's view—nobody referred to it as an act of purchasing or buying of one person by another. For most of the European missionaries the customary gifts by the future husband for his prospective wife and her family were not on par with "buying" the future bride. They therefore preferred to speak of "morning gift" and not of "bride price". The notion that marriage also had an economic side was not completely foreign to many of the missionaries and their South Western German or Swiss background: bride and groom were to bring some goods into a marriage. The reasoning that marriage was not equivalent to buying a person was based on the price for slaves, which was much higher than what a potential husband had to give to his future wife and her family. This can also be deduced from the sums mentioned in Aldinger's report: Wilhelmine Wulff and her family received $ 28 (= £7, s.b.), whereas the prize of a slave was almost double that amount: $ 50 (=£12 10s, s.b.).

Finally Aldinger's list also allows us insight into the purchasing power of Basel Mission salaries and wages at the time. Wilhelmine Wulff's remuneration as a teacher was £1 per month.[14] Some simple arithmetic on the basis of the information provided by missionary Aldinger results in the following equivalent: $1 = 80 strings; 16 strings = 1s → 5s = $1. Then there were $4 to £1—or 320 strings. One can then start to fill a virtual basket with the goods on offer, e.g. with 21 chickens. One can also wonder whether Wilhelmine's family had concluded that it would be better to take up the oppurtinity presented by the British commanding officer of Christiansborg, instead of the remuneration provided by the Basel Mission.

1   Archives of Mission 21, holdings of the Basel Mission (ABM), D-1.10 Odumase no.7—Carl Aldinger, Christiansborg 07.05.1859. Aldinger was on transfer from Abokobi, where he had been stationed in order to learn the Ga-language, to Odumase (Krobo). The months in between he spent in Christiansborg/Osu.

2   Peter Haenger, *Slaves and Slave Holders on the Gold Coast: Towards an Understanding of Social Bondage in West Africa* (Basel: P. Schlettwein Publishing, 2000), 28–9. Haenger quotes from the memorandum of John DeGraft-Johnson on domestic slavery dating from 1927.

3   Cati Coe, 'How Debt Became Care: Child Pawning and its Transformations in Akuapem, the Gold Coast, 1874–1929', *Africa* 82 (2012).

4   Marion Johnson, 'The Cowrie Currencies of West Africa: Part I', *The Journal of African History* 11, no. 1 (1970): 35.

5   Aldinger refers to various types of coins, but somewhat surprisingly does not mention any of Danish origin, although until 1850 Christiansborg belonged to Denmark.

6   Marion Johnson comes to the conclusion that the ban on the use of the cowrie shell as a currency in Asante at the beginning of the nineteenth century was not as strict it appears to have been by mid-century (Johnson, 1970: 37–8).

7   Hawanti refers to the town Ahabante. Some of the earliest Basel Mission stations on the Gold Coast were located in Akuapem.

8   One string contains 40 cowries.

9   Marion Johnson, 'The Cowrie Currencies of West Africa: Part II', *The Journal of African History* 11, no. 3 (1970): 338. Johnson describes the great inflation of the cowrie currency in Accra since the early 1850s, which led to its discontinuation in the 1870s.

10   Mary Esther Kropp Dakubu, 'The Portuguese Language on the Gold Coast, 1471–1807', *Ghana Journal of Linguistics* 1, no. 1 (2012): 26.

11   A photograph 'Counting Cowries' taken in Christiansborg by Christoph Wilhelm Locher in the early 1860s can be found in the Mission21/Basel Mission image archive under the signature 'QD-30.011.0068'. (see page 40)

12   One Florin (fl.) or Guilder was worth 60 Kreuzer.

13   ABM, D-1,10 Christiansborg no. 43, Quarterly report by missionary Wilhelm Locher for December 1858 to April 1859.

14   ABM, D-1,10 Christiansborg no. 4, Catherina Ruedi, Financial account (Rechnung) of the Girls' Boarding School for 1858–1859.

Paul Jenkins

Notes on the Basel Mission's Production of Knowledge in the Kannada Language in Nineteenth Century South India

A statue as starting-point

Half way along one of the main streets of Bangalore—MGR, Mahatma Gandhi Road—a life-sized statue stands on a plinth in a small municipal garden. Across the road a Hindu temple's roof is decorated with many colourful three-dimensional ladies, Krishna's milk-maids, perhaps. But the statue is sober and done in black metal. A German pastor in his preaching robes stands, with his hand resting on a large volume lying on an occasional table. 'It's the Bible', you might think. But go closer. A plaque in your language tells you that the statue represents the Basel missionary Ferdinand Kittel (1832–1903) and celebrates not a Bible translation, but his massive *Kannada-English Dictionary*.[1] But the plaque does not tell you that the statue was the brainchild of an ecumenical committee of distinguished Kannadiga scholars, Protestant, Catholic, and Hindu.

There have, of course, been many missionary linguists whose memory is treasured by the speakers of the language they investigated. But looked at comparatively, within the history of the Basel Mission, this statue (and its parallel in the Kerala town of Talasari depicting Hermann Gundert, the Mission's key nineteenth century authority on the Malayalam language) points at something unusually significant. Everywhere else where Basel Mission linguists codified and developed important regional languages or dialects—Southern Ghana, Cameroon, South China—these are now never more than popular carriers of oral culture inside and outside the church, and sometimes not even that. In contrast, in a reorganisation of the union states in South India carried through in 1956, Kannada and Malayalam became the official languages of Karnataka[2] and Kerala, states set up as entities for the speakers of these two languages.

As so often in India, there is also a simple but striking statistic to absorb. The number of native speakers of Kannada is usually given as something in the order of 35–40 million, a shade more than the population of that well-known North American homonym, the sovereign political state of Canada. It behoves us in the rest of the world to be far more aware of Karnataka than most of us are. Considering not only the population statistics but also Bangalore's status as a centre of technological innovation it is clear that, with Kannada, the Basel Mission was working in the nineteenth century on the mother-tongue of people of a considerable future prominence. And since Ferdinand Kittel's reputation is so high and general even outside the circles of the Christian community in Karnataka the Basel Mission's involvement with the Kannada language has contributed a lot to its general acceptance in a state in which Hindus form the large majority.

Basel Mission publications in Kannada

It is possible to be too dominated by the history of Bible translations and liturgical development when looking at missionary language policy and achievements. Take a couple of steps backwards and other dimensions may become visible. In the case of the Basel Mission and the Kannada language there is the campaign of a lexicographer and literary scholar like Kittel to study the whole available history of Kannada literature and to write about its words with etymological thoroughness, not least sorting out its Dravidian and Sanskrit roots. Kittel also achieved a codification of Kannada's dialect variations (Karnataka's longest dimensions are 750 km North-South and 400 km East-West, and the state includes two very dissimilar geographical zones, a coastal plain and a high plateau).

Beyond that Basel Mission linguists were also clearly engaged in developing languages 'so that', as Kittel's "Ghanaian" colleague J. G. Christaller put it, 'every thing worth to be known by educated men may be duly and fitly expressed in [the people's] own tongue ...' (in Christaller's case, Akan or Twi).[3] They were aiming to develop knowledge in vernacular languages, and that aim was especially vigorously pursued in South India. Already in the 1840s the Basel Mission had lithographical presses to produce materials in the Kannada and Malayalam scripts. In the 1850s a set of letter-press types for Kannada (produced by the *Schriftgiesserei* Haas in Basel, which had a long experience of printing in non-western alphabets) was exported to the Basel Mission Press in Mangalore,[4] which soon developed its own workshop for producing types. The Basel Mission Press was probably the leading press for the Kannada language up to the First World War, and also functioned as a publisher for the Basel Mission in Kannada.

The vagaries of twentieth century Basel Mission history in India mean, however, that reconstructing the production history of the Basel Mission Press in Mangalore—and thus studying a major part of the missionary production of knowledge in the Kannada language—is not easy. The Basel Mission's nineteenth century regulations included the instruction that each mission station should keep an archive with a proper collection of the past correspondence, of which each new missionary generation should be made aware. By the same token, a reference collection of the Press' productions was probably kept in Mangalore. But when the Basel Mission was progressively expelled from India during and immediately after the First World War its administrative structure collapsed, and no reference collection of Basel Mission publications in this language or Malayalam has survived. The printed pre-1914 Basel Mission Annual Reports in German and English do list productions of the Basel Mission Press in Mangalore, but one would like to be able to check them for comprehensiveness against an actual collection of the publications themselves. Instead, the only reference collection of Kannada publications—about 13 shelf metres in length—is to be found in the Basel Mission Archive, in Basel.

A collection like that is evidently a headache for an archivist in a city with no Indological tradition, and it is worth tracing the steps which have led to the production of a digital catalogue of Basel Mission's publications in Kannada. One major moving spirit was Srinavas Havanur. He was an academic and publicist and the leading authority on Kannada language and literature in his generation. He was also a Brahmin who, with a twinkle in his eye, used to claim he must have been a missionary in a former life, since he admired the missionaries' linguistic work so much. Havanur used every opportunity when he visited Europe to come to the Basel Mission archive, study the Kannada publications, and impress on the archivist the importance of the Basel Mission in the literary history of his language. Malini Jathanna, who stayed in Basel with her children during her husband's work on his doctoral degree in the late 1970s here, then undertook the work of creating a proper index of each item in this collection with her Kannadiga eye, typing the details of each on an A-5 sheet as far as this could be done in the Latin script, but adding the Kannada titles in her own handwriting. In the mid-1990s the Basel Mission librarian, Marcus Buess, obtained Swiss government money to microfilm the holdings of printed materials in Kannada and Malayalam as a conservation measure, which enabled us to deposit a copy of the microfilm in the Karnataka Theological College archive Mangalore, along with a copy of Mrs Jathanna's catalogue.[5] Using this gift from Basel, Havanur—who at that stage had retired and had been invited to live and work on the College campus—produced, together with the College Archivist Benet Amana, a proper digital catalogue of all the publications they could source, a compilation of some 1,000 titles.[6]

Knowledge production and the Basel Mission's Kannada publications to approximately the First World War

The shelving arrangement of the Kannada publications in the Basel Mission archive allows a crude thematic quantification (the statistics are to be understood as round figures):

Bible translations & theology	c. 200 items
Literature for congregational life (hymn books etc)	c. 150 items
Publications for schools	c. 525 items
(including a large number of titles which the Press printed for	
Government or publishers like Longmans or Macmillan)	
Dictionaries and grammars	c. 70 items
Tracts for distribution	c. 140 items
Miscellaneous	c. 110 items

Clearly someone who does not read Kannada cannot begin to assess the full importance of the knowledge production[7] which this effort at publishing achieved. Also, clearly, the major Basel Mission effort in this knowledge production was devoted to the Bible, theology, and support for evangelism. But this short paper attempts to raise one or two of the kinds of issues which come up when thinking about the Basel Mission in India against the background of publications and research on the missionary production of knowledge about Africa.

1. *Linguistics*   Patrick Harries' pioneer work on missionaries and the development of knowledge about Africa has stressed their involvement in research in the
natural sciences and anthropology.[8] Anthropology is missing in these Basel Mission
publications in Kannada—and replaced, as already hinted, by an important body of
publications on Kannada as language, but also as a literary tradition. Indeed, this area
of production not only included new works authored by missionaries like Ferdinand
Kittel. Kannadiga readers appreciated not least the Basel Mission's carefully edited
publications of ancient Kannada works about rhetoric in the language, and the
language's grammar. These can be regarded as the *production* of knowledge, since
"publication" here, of course, includes their appearance in potentially unlimited
quantities in print, where up to that point they had been circulating only in palm-leaf
manuscripts. "Edited" means that work had been done collating manuscripts of varying
quality in order to establish a convincing "best text".[9]

2. *Science*   The natural sciences, however we define the term, will tend to fall under
'Publications for schools' in the shelf order in Basel, though small publications for adult
education come under 'Tracts' and there is one very notable semi-publication of scientific
interest (see below), *Nature's Self-Printing*, under 'Miscellaneous'. A further and nar-
rower quantitative overview of publications relevant to the sciences and based on the
Havanur-Amana Catalogue is attached as Table One. From this it will be apparent that
the Basel Mission's production of scientific knowledge in Kannada was limited.

We should note, however, that there are three very substantial Basel Mission
contributions to knowledge of botany in Kannada:

• Hunziker, J., *Nature's Self-Printing, a series of useful and ornamental plants of the South Indian flora [...] taken
from fresh specimens in facsimile colours, botanautographed and published by J. Hunziker Basel Mission Press [...] 1862.*
This is a large-format two-volume production in which plant leaves have been treated with colour and then pressed
on fine paper to give an impression of their shape, structure and colour. At the bottom of each page the Latin name
of the plant is given, plus its name in a number of Indian languages, including Kannada. (I refer to this as a semi-
publication. About 20 copies seem to have been produced, not all with the identical number of pages.)
• Stolz, C., *Sahasraarda Vrukshandigala Vamane / Five Hundred Indian Plants, their use in Medicine and the Arts*
(235 pp., 1881, no illustrations).
This is a translation of the Linnaean system of plant classification into Kannada (pp. i–lvi) followed by detailed
descriptions in Kannada of individual plants and their uses (pp. 1–230).
• Pfleiderer, I., transl. Rau, M. Gopal, *Hindudeshada Sasya Shaastravu* (106 pp., 1919)
This is almost certainly an adapted or translated version of Pfleiderer's *Glimpses into the Lives of Indian Plants* 206 pp.,
a richly illustrated, including colour plates, Mangalore 1908. A third edition was published in Mangalore in 1916.)

Pfleiderer is one of the two Basel missionaries known to me anywhere before 1914 who
can be said to have done substantial research in one of the natural sciences. He specialised in the study of mosses on the Western Ghats. He worked in conjunction with
scholars in Europe and remarks, somewhat smugly, that because of their naming policy
he has '50 moss-children [...] *Macromitrium Pfleidereri, Omaliodelphus Pfleidereri etc*'.[10]

The other publications in the field of science and mathematics are at the level of teaching and public education rather than research. The publications on mathematics are almost exclusively on arithmetic (though one nineteenth century publication does introduce scholars to Euclid[11]). About one-third of the "science" titles are about practical questions of health (vaccination![12]), and, at the end of the nineteenth century, the dangers of alcohol consumption. One pamphlet from the turn of the twentieth century gives an account of the homeopathic treatment of diseases.[13] The use of homeopathy was a lively issue among some Basel missionaries in Ghana, and perhaps this was the case in India too. Some missionaries in Ghana were not convinced by the new discoveries about the vector of malaria, and preferred homeopathic medicine to imbibing anti-malaria prophylaxis being prescribed on the basis of this new knowledge.[14]

3. *Geography and the scientific attempt to deconstruct Hindu systems of knowledge.* An important question arises, however, as to how one defines "science" for this kind of analysis, and what happens when one shifts the context from the Western academy to dialogue and dialectic at the grass-roots in India where many missionaries were consciously inserting knowledge into discourse in Kannada in a way which, they hoped, would be fruitful for their work. On the one side one could write about "science" as *the natural sciences as they came to be taught in European and North American, South African, Indian and Chinese schools and universities, based on developing classifications, observation in dialectic with self- and mutual criticism, and the experimental method.* In India, however, "science" could also be seen as anything which provided *a rational critique which could be applied to the deconstruction of knowledge systems based on Hindu/Brahminical learning and belief.* And this brings geography, and to a lesser degree history, into the focus of this discussion.

I first came across this issue when reading early Basel Mission reports about the missionaries' contacts as they travelled in the region around and to the north of Dharwad-Hubli, a continental, non-coastal landscape on the Deccan plateau. They record signs of acute Hindu curiosity about the missionaries' teaching in geography— primarily, it seems, because they had maps on which the island of Sri Lanka was clearly drawn. They found themselves often talking to people for whom Sri Lanka was the island to which a devil had taken Sita, Lord Ram's wife, and which Ram invaded to rescue her, aided by an army of monkeys.[15]

The missionaries' attempts to ban this story to the world of legend and fairy-tale were serious, but its success could be gauged, much later, in 2007, when the Indian central government quickly abandoned a plan to dredge a channel for ocean-going ships between the southern tip of India and the northern tip of Sri Lanka owing to the threat of acute opposition among Hindu nationalists. They were beginning to argue that this would disturb the remains of the bridge constructed by Lord Ram to get to Lanka, a chain of small islands and sandbanks known in the West as 'Adam's Bridge'—originally a Muslim name—and in India as 'Ram Sethu'.

Members of the Government's own Archaeological Commission had submitted an affidavit asserting that there is no evidence that there was ever a historical figure called Ram, and that Adam's Bridge/Ram Sethu shows no signs of having been constructed by human (or simian) agency and would therefore not need to be treated as an archaeological monument. But at the thought of another emotional Hindu nationalist campaign developing (like that which led to the destruction of a mosque in Ahodya allegedly built on Ram's birthplace) the Government hastened to withdraw its proposals and disavow its archaeologists—and there were a number of resignations among key scientific personnel.[16] This is, of course, an emphatic indication that the missionary effort to invalidate the conservative Hindu world-view through the application of scientific knowledge has had at best very limited success.

Blowback: How Indian readers' reception of western knowledge in their resistance to evangelisation weakened the Basel Mission "at home"

Blowback, *(noun), a process in which gases expand or travel* in a direction opposite the usual one, *especially through escape of pressure or delayed combustion.*[17]

This essay has attempted to communicate a sense of the possible parallels and non-parallels of the history of the Basel Mission's generation of knowledge through its Kannada publications in relation to studies of the missionary generation of knowledge for the Western academy in Africa. It turns now in conclusion to look briefly at the reverse process, at the impact on the Basel Mission of the Indian reception of knowledge which could be used in the course of resistance to evangelisation. It incorporates, in an ironical way, that new cliché of missionary public relations, that 'the message is now being brought back to us' (*die Botschaft kommt zurück*). Nowadays this is usually used internally regarding the intended impact on lukewarm Christian circles in Europe of the more energetic and certain piety of Christian circles founded in the non-Western world by a couple of centuries of protestant evangelisation. But it can be used in a broader sense as well—looking at the general impact of ideas and cultural elements from Africa and Asia on the West, and the way they have helped dissolve a certain bourgeois moralist set of certainties characteristic of the Europe which is the background of the classical missionary movement and the high colonial period.[18]

With the nineteenth century Basel Mission, however, we can actually see in a specific case that the missionary attack on non-Christian religions resulted in a type of intellectual opposition in India which missionaries evidently found difficult to counter. And when training to preach against that particular kind of resistance came to be included in the syllabus of the Missionary College in Basel, it turned out that broad swathes of Basel Mission supporters felt betrayed in their conservative understanding of the faith they thought they shared with the missionaries.

The "elephant in the room" which caused this difficulty was the so-called historical-critical method in reading the Bible, especially the Gospels. This was an attempt pioneered by David Friedrich Strauss to write the life of Jesus as a modern historian would, identifying different traditions in the Gospels and the discrepancies one can find in them, and collating them to produce a much more realistic and less hagiographical biography of the historical Jesus.

The *locus classicus* for the impact of these ideas in India is the public debate before Western and Islamic judges in Agra in 1854 between a Basel-trained missionary of the Church Mission Society (CMS), C. G. Pfander, and the Islamic theologian Rahmat Alla al-Kairanawi. It seems plausible that Al-Kairanawi decided to attack Pfander because with his attractive style of writing in Urdu he was beginning to awaken attention among the Muslims of North India. Al-Kairanawi's support group included students or ex-students of the University of Calcutta who were aware of the English translation of Strauss' *Leben Jesu* and suggested questions and Bible quotations for the debate liable to lead to difficulties for Pfander. And, indeed, it seems that Pfander had not concerned himself with Strauss and found it difficult to counter Muslim arguments based on his writings. The debate was broken off and the Muslim side felt they had won.[19]

Exactly how the news of this Agra debate reached Basel, and when its impact began to be felt in the training given to future missionaries there, is not yet clear. Nor is it clear whether discussions and publications in the Kannada language reflected this general problem for Christian apologetics. (Since Urdu was both the language used by Pfander and the language of Muslim soldiers in garrison towns like Bangalore, and since there are indigenous Muslim groups in south-western India, the Maplas, it seems quite plausible that news of the Agra debate may have reached Kannadiga ears.) By the 1890s, however, whether or not South India was included in the loop of Basel Mission concern about knowledge of the historical-critical method among Indian critics of Christian missions, it is clear that students in the Missionary College were being led through a contemplation of this style of reading the Bible by the College's Rector, in order to prepare them for confrontations in Indian and Chinese cities. His lectures were well-enough worked out for them to be published in 1894.[20] But then hostile criticism developed in the Basel Mission's "home base". Bible-based Pietists were unhappy as they realised that this sceptical style of Bible reading was being taught in a fortress of proper Pietist faith. Opposition was expressed openly. And—we have the problem that there is no broad recent research into the history of the nineteenth century Basel Mission at home—it appears that this was the first moment when the wide protestant support for the Basel Mission in South-Western Germany and German-speaking Switzerland suffered a major split. It seems no coincidence that what became the Liebenzell Mission, which committed itself to a literal reading of the Bible, was being founded in the Basel Mission's home region at this time, winning over a notable proportion of the Basel Mission's grassroots support.

Shami Chakrabati, a lady of Indian origins, is a prominent human rights activist in Great Britain, appears frequently on serious TV channels commenting on human rights issues in Britain, and was chosen as one of the bearers of the Olympic banner at the opening of the London Games in 2012. As someone from the realm of the former Raj who now represents British liberal idealism in Great Britain itself she is an important symbol for what can happen in the Empire's post-imperial phase.

In a—for liberals, if not for Tories—benign way she post-figures the "blowback" mechanism I have suggested that India was capable of generating as early as the end of the nineteenth century.

From a European perspective the Basel Mission must have looked a very well-found and secure body at that time. In fact it was not only threatened in its immediate future by the coming clash of European nationalisms, and in the middle distance by the rise of anti-colonial nationalisms. In Asia it was already suffering from intellectual marginalisation. In the competition to generate knowledge it was by no means having things all its own way.

Approximate number of Basel Mission publications on specific themes in Kannada to 1914 (based on the Havanur-Amana catalogue)[21]:

	Pub. Before 1850	1850–74	1875–99	1900–14	Total >1914
Geography					
<100 pp		4	6	2	17
>100 pp	1	1	1	2	
History					
<100 pp		3	4	2	16
>100 pp		1	3	3	
Maths (all branches, 19th Century predominantly arithmetic)					
<100 pp		4	13	1	24
>100 pp		3	2	1	
Science (including publications on health)					
<100 pp			10	4	19
>100 pp			4	1	

An unsolved problem concerns the Basel Mission responsibility for the contents of the publications registered here and its responsibility for financing them. The Basel Mission Press (BMP) in Mangalore functioned partly as a printer producing books/pamphlets for other publishers—Government Education Departments in Mumbai and Chennai, for instance, or early commercial publishers in India ('Macmillan' and 'Longmans' appear in the catalogue especially in connection with schoolbooks). If the catalogue names a publisher which is not BMP, the case is clear. In all other cases it is assumed BMP was publisher, though little is known about the organisation and financing of the activities of BMP, so a certain residual doubt remains about this default ascription to BMP.

1 Ferdinand Kittel, *A Kannada-English Dictionary* (Mangalore: Basel Mission Book and Tract Depository, 1894), 1,752 pages. The Kannada language was formerly called 'Kanaresisch' in Basel Mission literature.
2 Initially Karnataka was named 'Mysore'. The present name was adopted in 1973.
3 From 'The Editor to the Readers…', in *Christian Reporter for the Natives of the Gold Coast speaking Twi or the Asante language*, 1893, 51–2.
4 These cases of type followed an epic route including crossing the Alps on the Gotthard Pass—see Jennifer Jenkins, 'Travelling to India in the 1850s. An account by Fanny Würth-Leitner, one of Ferdinand Kittel's travelling companions', in *A Dictionary with a Mission*, ed. William Madtha et al. (Mangalore: Karnataka Theological Research Institute, 1998).
5 Unfortunately the grant turned out not to be adequate for microfilming the whole body of materials, and about one-third of the Kannada holdings had to be omitted: apparently mostly those concerned with Bible translation, theology, and congregational literature.
6 The catalogue uses a Microsoft Works database capable of taking the Kannada and Latin scripts.
7 'Production'—this word is being used here in the sense of the work of a publisher rather than that of researchers. One could also use the word 'insertion' to describe the missionary effort to 'insert' exotic knowledge into (an) existing knowledge system(s).
8 Most recently in Patrick Harries and David Maxwell, eds., *The Spiritual in the Secular* (Grand Rapids: Eerdmans, 2012).
9 Particularly Ferdinand Kittel, ed., *Naagavarmana Kannada Chhandassu/A classical work in Kannada prosody* (Mangalore: Basel Mission Press, 1875), 401 pp.; Ferdinand Kittel, ed., *Hale Kannada Sankepa Vyaakarama/Short grammar of the ancient Kannada language* (Mangalore: Basel Mission Press, 1866), 104 pp.; Ferdinand Kittel, ed., Keshiraaja's *Shabdanianai-Darpanu/twelfth century 'mirror of grammar'* (Mangalore: Basel Mission Press, 1872), 420 pp.
10 Immanuel Pfleiderer, *Erinnerungen aus meinem Leben, geschrieben in den Nachkriegsjahren 1945–49* (Stuttgart, 2002), 164-6. The University Library catalogue in Basel indicates that Pfleiderer was also the author of a work with several hundred annotated botanical pictures—*Erläuterungen zu 384 Lichtbildern über Bau und Leben der Pflanzen* (1929). The other Basel missionary who was involved in processes of research recognised at a university level was Rudolf Fisch, the first scientifically trained Basel Mission doctor in Ghana, who has been the subject of modern studies by Hermann Friedrich Fischer, and Linda Ratschiller.

11 *Yuklidana Bhumitiya / Euclid's Geometry*, 1892. This was, however, not published by BMP but by the Bombay Government, which stresses once more the nineteenth century Basel Mission concentration on arithmetic in Kannada.
12 G. A. Nappaya, *Prashnottaravu / Catechism on Vaccination* (Mangalore: Basel Mission Press, 2nd ed. 1881), 16 pp.
13 *Homyopathi chikkitsaa musti / Treatment of common diseases by homeopathy* (Mangalore: Basel Mission Press, 1901), 74 pp.
14 Friedrich Hermann Fischer, *Der Missionsarzt Rudolf Fisch und die Anfänge medizinischer Arbeit der Basler Mission an der Goldküste (Ghana)* (Herzogenrath: Murken-Altrogge, 1991), 356–8. Reports on the difficulty of insisting on the use of quinine-prophylaxis among Basel missionaries in the early twentieth century because of the tendency of some of them to prefer herbal and homeopathic means to combat illness.
15 See translations into English of Basel Mission reports from N. Karnataka: Paul & Jennifer Jenkins, *Journeys and Encounters: Religion, Society and the Basel Mission in North Karnataka 1837–1852* (2013), accessed December 1, 2014, http://divinity-adhoc.library.yale.edu/BaselMission Karnataka. Here pp. 1.24, 3.34, 4.33 and 5.5.
16 The excellent Indian fortnightly *Frontline*—much read by NGO activists—devoted pp. 4–27 of its 5 October 2007 issue to this story.
17 *The New Oxford Dictionary of English* (Oxford: Clarendon Press, 1998), 192.
18 This is potentially a rich seam to mine: Think of the impact on the authority of the protestant Christian view of the world which Hermann Hesse—son and grandson of Basel missionaries—had through his propagation of Asiatic philosophy and literature. And, surely, if we think broadly enough, could we not see Jazz, with its ability to subvert the authority of classical Western culture, as West Africa's revenge on rigid missionary moralism?
19 I follow here the account and analysis of the Agra debate in Avril Powell, *Muslims and Missionaries in Pre-Mutiny India* (Richmond: Routledge, 1993). Powell reads Urdu, and was able to incorporate in her analysis the anti-Pfander pamphlets circulating in the mid-nineteenth century (and in some cases still in circulation as she did her research in the 1980s). The English translation of Strauss' *Leben Jesu* was done by George Eliot, and published in 1846.
20 Adolf Kinzler, *Über Recht und Unrecht der Bibelkritik: Zur Verständigung mit ängstlichen Verehrern der Bibel* (Basel: Reich, 1894).
21 This is an attempt to count the number of publications per subject area, but the figures are orders of magnitude only.

Tanja Hammel

Of Birds and (Wo)Men

Blue and reddish-brown birds fly over the land. Occasionally the jay-sized birds sit on a rock or the backs of cattle. The cavity-nesting birds winter in dry, wooded savannah or bushy African plains. These European rollers feed on beetles, crickets, locusts, caterpillars, flies, spiders, frogs, lizards, snakes, and weak, small birds. They circulate above farmhouses in Albany, the Eastern Cape, where they captivated me on my last visit in April 2014. They also fascinated Mary Elizabeth Barber (née Bowker), who was born in England in 1818 and settled in Albany at the eastern frontier of the Cape Colony with her family as a two-year-old. Soon after arrival, her family established the farm *Tharfield* across the Kleinemond River, about thirteen kilometres east of Port Alfred. In the 1860s, the birds mesmerised Barber so much that she became one of the main correspondents of Edgar Leopold Layard (1855–1872), curator of the South African Museum. Many passages from her letters were later published in Layard's *The Birds of South Africa* (1867), the first definitive account of South African birds. She was the only woman quoted.[1] At that time, European and American men still predominated the comparatively recent discipline of ornithology (1820–1850).

Misunderstanding ornithology as an 'inconsequential, even, apolitical'[2] science, historians have paid it little attention. Patrick Harries, however, saw its potential and encouraged me to dig deeper when I had a presentation during which I introduced a quotation in which Barber directly compared and contrasted human and avian couples' monogamy and lifelong fidelity and harmony with each other:

> Many species of birds, [...] choose their mates once and for all, and they live together (provided no accident occurs to either sex) through the natural term of their lives, in such cases there is but little display on the part of the males of fine feathers, or singing to enchant the females; such birds pursue the even tenor of their way as do married people of the human race, displaying, however, great affection for each other, which is not always the case on the part of human beings.[3]

Birds were Barber's 'companions', her 'best friends' and allies in her struggle for egalitarian gender relations.[4] They allowed her to intervene in the iconic tradition of depicting monogamous domesticity and familial harmony in bird illustrations in the 1860s and 1870s. The discussion was primarily one among ornithologists such as John Gould and their subscribers from the conservative gentry.[5] Illustrations in Gould's publications served to show females next to their nests, incubating, protecting and feeding, hovering over their offspring, while males were standing or perching to the side.

Barber ridiculed male chauvinistic behaviour, paternalistic characteristics and gendered labour division,[6] depicted couples standing on equal levels as well as two birds of the same sex in a nest. She was particularly interested in birds with slight sexual dimorphism, hardly visible differences such as the female's slightly smaller size, shorter wings, bill, crest and slight alteration in colour, as in *Coracias garrula* Linn., the European rollers.

Barber stressed egalitarian gender arrangements by showing how the male birds shared responsibilities in rearing the young.[7] Her criticism stemmed from first-hand negative experiences with matrimony and child rearing that raised her awareness for the timely need for women's equal rights. This requirement made her one of the first at the Cape to support sexual selection—the theory that remained mostly ignored for more than a century[8]—that she saw as a potential help to liberate women.[9]

Her strong statements indicate that she was criticising the conservative Victorian ideal of womanhood and pleading for women's rights. She was living in a strong patriarchal society that, according to Beatrice Hicks, who lived and worked in the Eastern Cape as a teacher from 1894 to 1897, was much worse than in England.[10] The analysis of Barber's contributions to ornithology allows us to gain much insight into science and society at the Cape.

While Patrick saw this potential and recommended I write about Barber, she has only featured in his work in a side-comment.[11] Women have been as absent in his texts as black women were in the mining areas in the immediate vicinity of Johannesburg in the late 1890s.[12] In the rare cases where women are mentioned, their examples serve to illustrate women's peculiar understanding of science, a male sphere with inaccessible practices. Patrick mentions Hanna Bohner, Basel missionary wife in Cameroon, who reported on her collecting "vermin" for entomologists[13] and Sarah Frances Colenso's conviction that entomology was an adequate leisure activity for upper class girls but a distraction for boys from the 'serious things in life'.[14] 'Science', as Ann Harries made clear, was a 'manly pursuit' and 'no place for a lady'.[15]

Patrick's focus on men allowed him to make major contributions to masculinity studies. His articles range from his study of southern Mozambican mine workers' male-male sexuality, a *rite de passage* facilitating the construction of manliness to the Alpine peaks as a 'testing ground for masculinity' and 'a symbol of man's domination over the land'.[16] 'Arriving at the University of Cape Town in 1972, [he] was caught up in a male string of arguments', Patrick says, and to this very day he has remained so.[17] While I am glad Patrick and his colleagues left for us so much work on women to be done, his studies on men's science in southern Africa inspire my attempt at an alternative view on knowledge production at the Cape.

As American author Joan Walsh Anglund wisely put it: 'a bird doesn't sing because it has an answer, it sings because it has a song'.[19] For "the lyrics" I am currently writing, I learned much from Patrick's 'Dance to the Music of Time', particularly from his important contributions to the social history of science in southern Africa that have also inspired studies on postcolonial Switzerland.[18] I wonder what Patrick's future songs will be about. He raised high expectations in his farewell lecture when he mentioned that Henri Alexandre Junod only produced his very good work in retirement.

1   Edgar Leopold Layard, Further Notes on South-African Ornithology, *The Ibis*. New Series XX: XXXII (1869), 74, 77, 365, 366, 370, 371, 373–374; Richard Bowdler Sharpe (ed.), *The Birds of South Africa by Edgar Leopold Layard* (London: Bernard Quaritch, 1875–1884), 150, 708, 782, 797; Layard mentioned Mrs. van Zyl's ridiculing description of her encounter with the 'coward' 'little Frenchman' Francois Le Vaillant (1753–1824) in a lengthy footnote and acknowledged Miss Boonzaier of Hoedtje's Bay for the donation of a *Phoenicopterus erythraeus* egg.

2   Nancy Jacobs, 'The Intimate Politics of Ornithology in Colonial Africa', *Comparative Studies in Society and History* 48:3 (2006), 565.

3   Mary Elizabeth Barber, 'On the Peculiar Colours of Animals in Relation to Habits of Life', *Transactions of the South African Philosophical Society* 4 (1878), 30–31. She had written the paper in 'such a dull uninteresting old place' and required Trimen's help in classification for it, Royal Entomological Society, St Albans, Trimen Correspondence, Box 18, Letter 101, Barber to Trimen, Kimberley, 2 November 1877.

4   Barber to Joseph Dalton Hooker, Kew Library, Art & Archives, Director's Correspondence, vol. 189, 114, Highlands, 9 May 1867; Mary Elizabeth Barber, *A plea for insectivorous birds*, published by request (Grahamstown 1886), 3, 12.

5   See Jonathan Smith, 'Gender, Royalty, and Sexuality in John Gould's *Birds of Australia*', *Victorian Literature and Culture*, 35:2 (2007), 569–587; Jonathan Smith, 'Darwin's Birds', in Jonathan Smith, *Charles Darwin and Victorian Visual Culture* (Cambridge: Cambridge University Press, 2006), 92–136; Jonathan Smith, 'Picturing Sexual Selection. Gender and Evolution of Ornithological Illustration in Charles Darwin's *Descent of Man*', in Ann B. Shteir and Bernard V. Lightman ed. *Figuring It Out: Science, Gender, and Visual Culture* (Lebanon NH, Dartmouth College Press, 2006), 85–109.

6   Bowdler Sharpe (ed.), *The Birds of South Africa*, 240–241.

7   Bowdler Sharpe (ed.), *The Birds of South Africa*, 34–35; Barber, 'On the Peculiar Colours of Animals', 30.

8   See Paulo Gama Mota, 'Darwin's Sexual Selection Theory—a Forgotten Idea', *Anthropologia Portuguesa* 26/27 (2009/2010), 149–161.

9   She aimed for the paper's publication in England, as she believed many in the Cape Colony had not read Wallace's paper. Four months later, she sent the paper to Roland

Trimen in Cape Town, entomologist and curator of the South African Museum as well as co-founder of the South African Philosophical Society. Library of the Royal Entomological Society, St Albans, Trimen Correspondence, Box 18, Letter 102, Barber to Trimen, Kimberley 26 November 1878.

10   See Fiona Fourie, 'A "New Woman" in the Eastern Cape', *English in Africa* 22:2 (1995), 70–88.

11   Patrick Harries, *Butterflies & Barbarians: Swiss Missionaries & Systems of Knowledge in South-East Africa* (Oxford etc.: James Currey etc., 2007), 142.

12   Patrick Harries, 'Symbols and Sexuality: Culture and Identity on the Early Witwatersrand Gold Mine', *Gender & History* 2, no. 3 (1990), 323. Patrick was by no means the only white South African historian of his generation neglecting women, as Helen Bradford has shown: See H. Bradford, 'Women, Gender and Colonialism: Rethinking the History of the British Cape Colony and Its Frontier Zones, c. 1806–1870', *Journal of African History* 37 (1996), 351–370; —, 'Peasants, Historians, and Gender: A South African Case Study Revisited, 1850–1886', *History and Theory* 39 (2000), 86–110.

13   Patrick Harries, 'Natural Science and Naturvölker: Missionary Entomology and Botany', in *The Spiritual and the Secular. Missionaries and Knowledge about Africa*, ed. Patrick Harries and David Maxwell (Grand Rapids, MI: William B. Eerdmans Publishing Company, 2012), 53–54.

14   Harries, 'Natural Science and Naturvölker', 55.

15   Ann Harries, *Manly Pursuits* (London: Bloomsbury Publishing PLC, 1999); Ann Harries, *No Place for a Lady* (London: Bloomsbury Publishing PLC, 2007).

16   Harries, Symbols and Sexuality, 318–336; —, 'From the Alps to Africa. Swiss Missionaries and Anthropology', in H. Tilley (ed.), *Ordering Africa. Anthropology, European Imperialism and the Politics of Knowledge* (Manchester: Manchester University Press, 2007), 206.

17   Patrick Harries' Farewell Lecture: 'History and Anthropology: A Dance to the Music of Time', 11 December 2014.

18   See e.g. Patricia Purtschert, Barbara Lüthi and Francesca Falk (eds.), *Postkoloniale Schweiz: Formen und Folgen eines Kolonialismus ohne Kolonien* (Bielefeld: transcript, 2012). *Butterflies and Barbarians* (2007) and the article 'From the Alps to Africa. Swiss Missionaries and Anthropology' (2007) influenced the field.

19   Joan Walsh Aglund, *A Cup of Sun* (city unknown: Harcourt, 1967), 15.

Patrick Grogan

German Natural History Collectors and the Appropriation of Human Skulls and Skeletons in Early Nineteenth Century Southern Africa: Towards a Discursive Analysis of Collecting

As Patrick Harries has shown in his article 'Warfare, Commerce and Science: Racial Biology in South Africa',[1] the collecting of human skulls, skeletons, and other bodily remains was a not uncommon practice in the early nineteenth century Cape Colony. Patrick provides an important overview of this dubious activity, describing the transnational networks of trade, warfare, and supposed scientific knowledge which drove it, as well as identifying the collectors in the field responsible for its dirty work. As the title of his article suggests, Patrick argues that commerce ultimately fed off warfare—in this case, 'the violence on the [Cape's eastern] frontier'[2]—to provide a supply of human specimens for nascent racial scientists to pore over and from which to test their hypotheses. My own interest in the topic had already been awoken through my ongoing doctoral research on early nineteenth century German naturalist-collectors in southern Africa[3], including many of those, like Hinrich Lichtenstein and Ludwig Krebs, whom Patrick mentioned. As is apparent in his article and as has become obvious to me through my own research, German collectors—who are often referred to, and indeed tended to refer to themselves, simply as naturalists—were also actively involved in the collecting, storing, and trading or donating of human skulls, skeletons, and even preserved flesh, adopting in the process the same methods and techniques of storage and preservation as for their other mammal finds. In this short paper, I want to suggest a potentially fruitful avenue for further research on the topic through a necessarily brief textual analysis of written accounts of human skull and skeleton collecting by three German naturalist-collectors active in early nineteenth century southern Africa.

In the first half of the nineteenth century, particularly after Britain took control of the territory in 1806, the Cape Colony was an accessible and favoured destination for collectors of natural history specimens from all over Europe. Germans were among the most common collectors, usually active both within the colony and beyond its borders. Three of the most prolific of these from this period were Hinrich Lichtenstein (1780–1857), Ludwig Krebs (1792–1844) and Carl Friedrich Drège (1791–1867). Lichtenstein was the archetypical amateur collector who collected in his spare time while in the employ of the Cape's Batavian governors, later donating his collections to various European scientific institutions. In contrast, Krebs and Drège represented a brand of commercial collectors who, by the 1820s, came to dominate the collecting enterprise at the Cape. The former was employed by the Berlin Zoological Museum—directed at the time by Lichtenstein—with the express purpose to provide it with specimens, the latter a self-employed collector who would regularly auction off or sell his collections to fund further collecting expeditions.[4]

As Patrick notes, the demand for human specimens in early nineteenth century Europe was high due to the growing scientific interest in the study of comparative anatomy. This had become an influential scientific discipline in its own right, as renowned metropolitan comparative anatomists such as Georges Cuvier in Paris and Johann Friedrich Blumenbach in Göttingen were developing theories of racial difference.[5] Moreover, the sub-disciplines of phrenology and craniology were about to take off as supposedly legitimate sciences, the further study of which required more and more specimens from around the world for experiments and analyses. Thus, with a ready interest in and market for human specimens in Europe, the task for the likes of Lichtenstein, Krebs and Drège at the Cape was simply to find appropriate specimens.

Lichtenstein, during the course of his travels around the colony, toured its northern frontier, a site of frequent conflict between Dutch farmer commandos and the so-called "Bushmen". "Bushman" skulls were particularly sought-after by comparative anatomists as they were viewed as archaic remnant from the primitive days of mankind, and thus ideal for comparison with supposedly modern Europeans. Lichtenstein was thus keen to claim a "Bushman" skull as a specimen and records a very vivid description of his efforts to do so:

> The solitary situation of this [farm] has, besides, [the] disadvantage, that it is with much more difficulty defended against Bosjesmans [Bushmen] and the wild beasts, both of which are of course the more abundant in proportion as the country is destitute of other inhabitants. The neighbourhood of this farm is often the theatre of terrible strifes with the Bosjemans: and Van Aschwege related to me with great simplicity, as a matter of perfect indifference, that at only a few hour's distance, lying out in the open fields, were the skeletons of some Bosjemans, who had been shot a few years before by the owner of the place, as they were stealing some of his oxen. Long as I had been anxious to secure the skull of some of these remarkable people, I entreated our host to permit some of his slaves or Hottentots to go and fetch me one of the skulls, for which I would give them something to drink: to this he willingly consented but neither menaces or entreaties could prevail on any of them to earn the promised recompense. They declared that they would rather carry the heaviest burden all the way from Graaf Reynett, than the head of a dead man the distance of only a quarter of an hour [...] All I could obtain was that one of the slaves should accompany me to the place where the skeletons were lying; for this service he would not however accept any money, but begged of me some article of old cloathing. At the place indicated, I found the bones of, as I supposed, about four men, but the carcases had been so torn, gnawed and scattered about by the wild beasts, that I could with great difficulty find among the fragments parts of two skulls: these for want of better specimens, I was forced to carry away with me as a great treasure. My conductor stopped at some distance, where he remained until I returned to him, nor would he offer to carry my burden for me a single step of the way.[6]

Meanwhile, for Ludwig Krebs, the Sixth Frontier War (1834–1835), some three decades after Lichtenstein's stay in the colony, provided an opportunity to collect his own specimens. Recalling in a letter to Lichtenstein, now in his capacity as museum director in Berlin, how a colonial commando had killed twenty-two Xhosa warriors, Krebs's reaction had been to 'immediately [think] of fetching some of the bodies', a foray which resulted in finding 'all the skeletons destroyed by the hyenas except two heads; these I will send you'.[7] These had been a significant prize for Krebs, who professed a collector's appreciation for the 'beautiful, athletic bodies' of the Xhosa and had since his arrival at the Cape formed the goal of supplying Lichtenstein with a 'kaffir skull, or, if possible, a kaffir skeleton'. Indeed, he had already succeeded in doing this once before in 1821, claiming a Xhosa skull which possibly belonged to the prophet Makana, who had drowned while trying to escape from imprisonment on Robben Island and whose body was washed ashore near Cape Town. To the noticeable shock of his servants and slave, Krebs had 'thought immediately to obtain a scientific advantage out of this unhappy incident' and dug up the body:

> Only two bodies of a kaffir and a hottentot were washed ashore [...] the kaffir's body was mostly eaten by wild animals and [...] the head of the the hottentot was smashed on the rocks by the waves. [A fellow collector, Stadler] thought, however, that the head of the [other] kaffir was well preserved. He would dig this up for me. [...] After a good breakfast, which the kind daughter of Stadler had prepared for us, we went to work. Three slaves now began to dig, and I noticed with pleasure that the head was well-preserved, although the neck was already half-eaten. I decided immediately to separate it from the body. Those present, in particular the slaves, looked at me in horror! But I placed my conquest into a container and tied it up with a cloth.[8]

Carl Drège too was determined to obtain the skulls or skeletons of indigenous people at the Cape and was similarly prepared to break local taboos to claim them. When a "Bushman" woman was found dead near the expedition route, Drège moved quickly into action:

> Tonight it was cold, I found thick frost. All blossoms of the peach- und plum trees were frozen dead. Stormy. I cut only the bones und some flesh from the woman's corpse, during which a Briqua surprised me by appearing in front of me, but did not dare to come any closer. I hid the flesh and bones deep under stones and put the skin away late that evening into a sack in the waggon, having walked in a wide circle around the Briqua kraals.[9]

While Drège, unlike Lichtenstein and Krebs, made some attempt to conceal his actions—secretly digging up the body, wrapping the skull in a linen cloth and hiding it in his waggon—his disregard for local customs and the dignity of the dead is conspicuous. Although his writing style tended towards brevity throughout his journal, the jump from calm domesticity implicit in descriptions of the weather to a gruesome description of his efforts to skin the corpse is striking. Furthermore, as Rau remarks, Drège simply prepared this human specimen for preservation in the same manner as he did for all large mammals.[10] While Rau is correct to place these actions in the context of their time—an era in which public dissections of human cadavers in Europe were common—the dehumanising gaze of the vigilant collector always on the lookout for human specimens to place among his mammal, bird, reptile, amphibian, fish, insect, plant, and mineral collections is marked. Furthermore, it is telling how human specimens such as these sent by Krebs and Drège were described in auction catalogues in Germany, where they were often presented as one rarity for sale among many others from all spheres of nature.[11]

Whereas enthusiasm, excitement and collecting zeal mark the three collectors' accounts, horror, disgust and fear are said to overcome the locals. Unfortunately, we are limited in our understandings of these events by our reliance on the collectors' own narrative of events, but, still, from these we can gain a sense of the conflicting reactions to the practice of collecting human remains. Drège, anticipating local disapproval, attempts to ensure that he is unseen. Krebs describes the shock of his slaves, while Lichtenstein explores the matter in somewhat more depth:

> Towards evening a messenger arrived [...] This messenger was the same Hottentot who in the afternoon had remonstrated the most strongly against the expedition to seek the Bosjeman's skull. I asked him whether he was not afraid to go by night among all the lions and other beasts of prey? He answered, pointing to his gun, that he knew very well how to shoot a lion through the body, but against a dead man's head there was nothing to be done... I am inclined to think [...] that the germs of [these superstitious fears] lurk in the souls of even the wildest and must uncultivated part of mankind; and 'tis not a very small degree of cultivation that must be requisite, to divest a whole people of their prejudices with regard to the mysterious power attached to the remains of the human body.[12]

For Lichtenstein, these differing reactions are simply a result of science coming face to face with superstition. Analysed from a less subjective angle, however, we can see that the collectors, in their zeal to collect the new and the rare, were prepared to overstep the boundaries of acceptable behaviour to claim such sought-after specimens. As we would be today, the locals were shocked at such audacious disrespect for the dead. In her article on Victorian human skull collectors, Franey has argued that the 'secrecy and fetishization' displayed by collectors, as exhibited by Drege in our example, 'combine to give [the practice] a decidedly nonrationalist and magical feel'.[13] Indeed, for Franey, this secret act of collecting could be said to exude the very magical element from which self-proclaimed naturalist-collectors such as Drège sought to distance themselves.

Only in recent decades, with increasing efforts to repatriate human remains held in European museums to their countries of origin, has the imperative to reveal the broader context in which such collections were originally made received more attention from scholars. Hopefully, this all too short contribution serves to highlight a further avenue of interest when approaching the topic, namely the need to reveal the conflicts over meaning which lay at the very heart of the enterprise.

1   Patrick Harries, 'Warfare, Commerce and Science: Racial Biology in South Africa' in *The Invention of Race: Scientific and Popular Representations* ed. Nicolas Bancel et al. (London: Routledge, 2014), 170–184.

2   Ibid., 175.

3   My ongoing doctoral research on 'The Berlin-Cape Nexus: German Naturalists at the Cape in the Early Nineteenth Century' is supervised by Patrick Harries at the Basel Graduate School of History, University of Basel and is generously supported and funded by the Swiss National Science Foundation (SNSF).

4   For further biographical detail on Lichtenstein, Krebs, and Drège, see their relevant entries in H. F. Glen and G. Germishuizen, ed., *Botanical Exploration of Southern Africa—2nd Edition* (Cape Town: A. A. Balkema, 2010).

5   As Harries notes, Lichtenstein sent a human skull from the Cape to Blumenbach in Göttingen.

6   Hinrich Lichtenstein, *Travels in Southern Africa in the Years 1803, 1804, 1805, and 1806* (Cape Town, 1928/1930 [1812]—English translation from the German original), 492.

7   Ludwig Krebs to Hinrich Lichtenstein, ca. 1835, translated in Pamela Folliott and Richard Liversidge, *Ludwig Krebs. Cape Naturalist to the King of Prussia 1792–1844* (Cape Town: A. A. Balkema 1971), 95–96.

8   Krebs to Lichtenstein, 2.10.1822, translated in *Ibid.*, 23.

9   Diary of Carl Drège (transcription), 13.09.1829, pp.20–21, MSC 61, File 226, National Library of South Africa, Cape Town [my translation].

10   Reinhold Rau, 'Der Mainzer *Quagga*-Fötus', *Mainzer naturwissenschaftliches Archiv*, 42, 2004, 248.

11   See, for example, Hinrich Lichtenstein, *Verzeichniss einer Sammlung von Säugethieren und Vögeln aus dem Kaffernlande, nebst einer Käfer-Sammlung, welche am 14ten März 1842 durch den Königl. Gerichtlichen Auctions-Commissarius Rauch öffentlich meistbietend verkauft werden sollen.* (Berlin, 1842), 10.

12   Lichtenstein, *Travels in Southern Africa*, 493.

13   Laura Franey, 'Ethnographic Collecting and Travel: Blurring Boundaries, Forming a Discipline', *Victorian Literature and Culture*, 29, no.1 (2001): 219–239.

Melanie Eva Boehi

Who Cut Down Margaret Thatcher's Tree?

On several occasions of presenting my research about the history of the South African botanical complex, Patrick Harries inquired about the fate of a tree planted by Margaret Thatcher at the Kirstenbosch National Botanical Garden in Cape Town. This short piece is an attempt to satisfy Patrick's curiosity as well as to explore the fascinating topic of politicians' tree plantings by focussing on one particular person and tree.

The tree planting described in the following occurred when Margaret Thatcher visited Cape Town in May 1991. At a reception at Tuynhuys, the Cape Town office of the South African presidency, F. W. de Klerk bestowed the Order of Good Hope upon Thatcher. This medal was mostly given to foreign dignitaries for their merit in service of South African international relations. In her speech, Thatcher expressed pride in Britain's contribution to bring about political change. 'As candid friends we have urged the South African Government forward', Thatcher said, 'and as loyal friends we have striven to give South Africans the room and time to bring reform into effect'.[1] The nature of the Iron Lady's friendship is of course tainted by the criticism that she could have done more to bring apartheid to an end while she served as British prime minister from 1979 to 1990. In the name of free trade and constructive engagement, Thatcher steadfastly opposed boycotts and angered activists and the presidents of independent African states when she received P. W. Botha at Chequers in 1984. At the Vancouver Commonwealth Summit of 1987, she infamously called the African National Congress 'a typical terrorist organisation'.[2]

The name Tuynhuys—literally meaning "Garden House"—refers to the origin of the building on its site that served as a tool shed for the Dutch East India Company's garden. The building has since been renovated and enlarged numerous times and served different purposes, including as governmental guesthouse. It is thus a long time ago that anybody entering Tuynhuys lifted a spade to engage in horticultural work. Margaret Thatcher nonetheless did exactly that during her visit to Cape Town, though at a different site. During her stay she was invited to plant a tree at the Kirstenbosch National Botanical Garden. Photographs of the occasion show Thatcher wearing a blue jacket, black skirt and her signature-style pearl necklace and earrings with a spade in hand.[3]

This was by no means the first occasion on which she planted a tree. Her 'Engagement Diary' for a visit to Canberra on 30 June 1979, listed a 'Tree-planting in garden' (allocated 10 minutes) in between 'TV interview' (50 minutes) and 'Lunch' (80 minutes).[4] On 18 September 1982, she planted a tree at the Tokai Nuclear Power Station in Japan.[5] A glimpse at the archive of the Margaret Thatcher Foundation and an Internet search indicate that there were likely many more tree plantings, but unfortunately nobody systematically documented this act of power planting politics. Tree planting demonstrates more powerfully than any other ceremony the imagination of rooting and growth. While planting a tree is a strong symbol of belief in the future, the significance of the ceremony is strongest in the present.

A natural death

At Kirstenbosch, Margaret Thatcher planted an *Ocotea bullata* tree.[6] Commonly known in English as black stinkwood, this flowering tree is indigenous to the high forests of South Africa.[7] Healers use its bark to produce medicine and the wood is also highly valued for furniture production. *Ocotea bullata* has been over-exploited and is now protected. In 1991, Kirstenbosch did not have a black stinkwood tree growing in the garden and staff members therefore chose the tree for Thatcher's planting on a site above the Cycad Amphitheatre. The tree was grown from seed collected in the forest above Kirstenbosch where the species naturally occurs. The seed was sown in the nursery and at the time of planting the tree had grown to about 1,5m in height. A plaque was placed with the tree to commemorate its prominent planter.

Margaret Thatcher's black stinkwood tree did not live long. According to the current curator of Kirstenbosch, Philip le Roux, it died a natural death. Stinkwood trees naturally grow in forests and need the company of other trees for protection, they cannot stand on their own. Thatcher's tree was therefore planted close to a *Kiggelaria Africana* (wild peach) tree. The wild peach tree was blown over during a storm about three years after Thatcher's visit and the sudden exposure led to the black stinkwood's demise. The empty site was later filled with a *Celtis Africana* (white stinkwood) tree.

Garden rumours

With the tree, the plaque remembering the prominent visitor disappeared. However stories about Thatcher and her tree at Kirstenbosch persist. They belong more to the world of fiction than facts and provide us with insights into how people experience history as they relate to plants and the institution of the Kirstenbosch National Botanical Garden. One of these Kirstenbosch myths I have learned from Patrick. According to this legend, Margaret Thatcher planted a tree at Kirstenbosch which was cut down after the end of apartheid. However, given the reluctance to transform monuments in Cape Town's public spaces where colonial statues are continuously well looked after, a cutting by political order seems unlikely. Kirstenbosch itself includes a number of colonial monuments that were not discarded but more critically historicised. The most prominent of these is Van Riebeeck Hedge, declared a national monument in 1934, which has not been cut but equipped with a new critical storyboard. The story about the political felling of Margaret Thatcher's tree thus speaks more of imaginations, fears and desires of Kirstenbosch's public.

Kirstenbosch horticulturalist Phakamani m'Afrika Xaba (left) and PhD-student Melanie Boehi (right) in front of the *Celtis Africana* tree that grows at the site where Margaret Thatcher had planted an *Ocotea bullata* tree in 1991. Picture: Anna Vögeli, 14 September 2014.

Another rumour is that the choice of a stinkwood tree was a secret insult. Thatcher herself is said to have inquired about the selection. Afrikaans plant names are typically more empirical and direct than the English ones. When cut *Ocotea bullata* effuses an unpleasant odour; thus the Afrikaans name *stinkhout,* and in English: stinkwood. This anecdote shows that the symbolism of trees is just as ambiguous as the symbolism of flowers.[8] If focus is put on the medicinal and industrial value, the choice of an *Ocotea bullata* is perceived as a great honour. Highlighting the tree's malodorous quality shifts the meaning from distinction to insult. When used symbolically, trees and flowers are culturally accepted as carriers of meanings that are not fixed but constantly have to be reaffirmed through contextualisation.

Tree plantings in the post-apartheid period

Margaret Thatcher is not the only dignitary who, through a tree planting, was rooted in Kirstenbosch's soil. Many politicians and dignitaries were given this honour. Among them are Daniel arap Moi, president of Kenya, who planted a wild olive tree as 'a link between Kenya and South Africa' in 1992, European royals, and since the mid-1990s also South African politicians including Kader Asmal, Ronnie Kasrils and Nelson Rolihlahla Mandela.[9] Today the most prominently remembered visitor is the late former state president Nelson Mandela. He visited Kirstenbosch in August 1996 and planted a *Warburgia salutaris* (pepper-bark) tree close to the garden's main entrance. A board reminds visitors of the occasion and explains that '[j]ust as this tree has brought healing to the people of South Africa, so too has Nelson Mandela brought healing to our nation'. Together with a display of the cultivar named after him—Mandela's Gold—and a bust of Mandela, the tree is today a popular feature with visitors.

None of the politicians' tree planting would have been possible without the ground staff and horticulturalists who collected seeds, grew them in the nursery, prepared the planting site, polished the spade, provided instructions, and looked after the trees' wellbeing. The tree plantings show how vast and diverse the network is in which Kirstenbosch has functioned since its establishment in 1913, including among its actors politicians, horticulturalists, gardeners, botanists, managers, journalists, plants, trees and the weather. In this network, science, society and politics do not exist separately but are deeply intertwined. The functioning of this network, Kirstenbosch's relationship to the public and the history of work in the garden are at the core of my research on the South African botanical complex. I would like to sincerely thank Patrick not only for sharing the Thatcher anecdote (I am sorry the facts do not make as sensational a story as the fiction!), but generally also for his generous support throughout my studies.

1 'Speech on receiving the Order of Good Hope from President De Klerk. 15 May 1991', Margaret Thatcher Foundation, accessed 17 August 2014, www.margaretthatcher.org/document/108267.

2 'Press Conference at Vancouver Commonwealth Summit. 17 October 1987', Margaret Thatcher Foundation, accessed 17 August 2014, www.margaretthatcher.org/document/106948.

3 Photographs in the collection of Philip le Roux, accessed 15 August 2014.

4 'MT Engagement Diary. 30 June 1979', Margaret Thatcher Foundation, accessed 17 August 2014, www.margaretthatcher.org/document/112832.

5 'MT Engagement Diary. 18 September 1982', Margaret Thatcher Foundation, accessed 17 August 2014, www.margaretthatcher.org/document/124957.

6 Philip le Roux, interview by Melanie Boehi, Kirstenbosch, Cape Town, 15 August 2014.

7 Giles Mbambezeli, 'Ocotea bullata (Burch.) Baill', PlantZAfrica, accessed 17 August 2014, www.plantzafrica.com/plantnop/ocoteabull.htm.

8 Melanie Boehi, 'Flower diplomacy. The ambiguous symbolism of plants, gardens and botany in South Africa in the 20th and 21st centuries' (paper presented at the UWC Anthropology and Sociology departmental seminar, Cape Town, 10 September 2014).

9 Tos Wentzel, 'I shall return, says Arap Moi', Cape Argus, June 10, 1992. Unknown author, '"Slim", suinige tuin bied oplossing vir watertekort', Die Burger, 5 June 1997. John Yeld, 'Trees take roots as symbols of healing', Cape Argus, 9 September 1999.

Franziska Rüedi

'Reluctant Bonds': On the Role of Narrative in Post-Apartheid South Africa[1]

The German word *Vergangenheitsbewältigung* has no equivalent in the English language.[2] Literally translated as 'coming to terms with the past', it implies an active engagement [*Auseinandersetzung*] with a problematic aspect or a period of the past.[3] In South Africa, the Truth and Reconciliation Commission's (TRC) process of translating lived experience into narrative was geared towards producing historical catharsis. This process was deeply rooted in the project of nation-building, reconciliation and healing in post-apartheid South Africa. As Deborah Posel summarised, 'Exposure to the truth was to lay the basis for a national consensus about the past and how to overcome its legacy in the future'.[4] Posel further stressed that the final report of the TRC 'disabled the link between subject and object, agent and structure', leading to 'the increasingly familiar refrain among white South Africans [...] that somehow the system propelled itself'.[5] Culpability was attributed to individual perpetrators, whose agency was often overstated and frequently divorced from a broader understanding of modes of power and mechanisms of control. The experiences of the black majority were structured along the dual tropes of victims and heroes and folded into a national narrative of despair and final triumph.[6]

The TRC's emphasis on, and definition of, gross human rights violations foreground the spectacle and demoted the normalisation of routine violence of the everyday in narrative processes. Limited by its focus on the period between 1960 and 1994, the report paid little attention to the historical continuities and diverse impulses in the production of the political, social and economic order that underpinned the apartheid period. Gabeba Baderoon notes that first European settlers constructed their sense of 'belonging' through 'naming the people who preceded European settlement as profoundly *other*, as lacking in fit and significance'.[7] This process of othering certainly contributed towards laying the basis for the discourse of racial hierarchy and its production and articulation of spatial, social and political difference. The construction of racial divisions and hierarchies was translated into museological practices, as Patrick Harries stresses. Display of history and art were racialised, juxtaposing the construction of a 'primitive African culture' with the 'advanced culture of European and Asian peoples'.[8] Centuries of slavery, dispossession, colonialism and segregation produced a strange relation between intimacy and distance that shaped "race relations" in South Africa.[9] Leading to the fragmentation of lived experiences, it contributed towards undermining the capacity for empathy, 'the ability to share and understand the feelings and experiences of another', and it created an imaginative void.[10]

75

Despite efforts to produce a shared understanding of the past, South Africa remains a deeply divided country where racism and prejudice are solidly entrenched.[11] Recent surveys point towards a decrease in perceptions of, and a desire for, national unity and social cohesion across racial categories.[12] In its report published in 2014, the Institute for Justice and Reconciliation notes that 'in 2013 only half of white South Africans agreed that apartheid was an unjust, inhumane, criminal system and only a third agreed that it has resulted in the continuing poverty of black South Africans today. The vast majority of South Africans in other race groups agreed with these statements'.[13] This lack of historical consciousness is embedded in what T. O. Molefe calls the 'totalising effects of the transition period's concepts—of its reconciliation ideology'.[14] Stories reflecting the diversity of experiences thus remain frequently contested, rejected and unacknowledged by different sections of society.

On a national level, South Africa's emphasis on reconciliation and unity has forged strange marriages between antagonistic and contending narratives of the past. This attempt to create a shared understanding is expressed in public holidays such as Reconciliation Day on 16 December, which has very different historical meanings to different population groups. While for Afrikaner nationalists it signifies the victory of the Afrikaners over the Zulu army in the 'battle of blood river' (the Ncome river) in 1838, the date also signifies the formation of the armed wing of the African National Congress, uMkhonto weSizwe. Efforts by government to create a 'feel-good history'[15] has led to the emergence of statist narratives in public discourse that flatten the ambiguities of the struggle for freedom and the complexity of state control and power. While some experiences have been rendered unspeakable, others are willingly silenced in a stubborn refusal to engage with the complexity of past experiences.[16] Thus contrary to what Njabulo Ndebele optimistically foretold in 1998, narrative has only been restored to a limited extent.[17] With the recent death of Nelson Mandela and the 20th anniversary of the first democratic elections, public discourse on the role of the past in shaping the present has intensified. Yet as South Africans and the world celebrate twenty years of democracy, the abundance of stories reflecting the diversity of experiences Ndebele anticipated have only partly emerged.

The production of a statist narrative was recently highlighted during the 30th anniversary of the Vaal Uprising. Sparked by a series of rent increases, thousands of residents in the African townships of the Vaal Triangle marched on 3 September 1984 to protest against the political order and to express their deep-seated socio-economic grievances. The protests quickly translated into a sustained and violent uprising, heralding the beginning of the insurrectionary period of the mid-1980s. As I have argued elsewhere, popular protests not only demanded political rights, they also reflected a growing discourse and struggle over a new social and economic order.[18] Nationally, the day has been receiving very limited attention and no memorial site exists that commemorates the uprising of 1984. In his article on the commemoration, Mondli Makhanya refers to the absence of memorial sites, arguing that 'the areas where the revolt began are barren sites and give no idea that something historical happened there'.[19]

Commemorations and monuments speak to the spectacular events of the past, yet the routine violence of the everyday is imprinted with the 'inward and outwards signs' of past struggles, to borrow Gabeba Baderoon's term.[20] The visibility of inequality and poverty contrasts the socio-economic equality and justice local residents were struggling for in 1984. During a speech in 2012, one of the former Delmas Treason trialists who had been imprisoned for his involvement in the protests of 1984, stressed that 'the township looks exactly like it did before, when we took action against the Apartheid government'.[21] In 2014, public speeches by politicians commemorating the 30th anniversary paid tribute to the role of popular struggles in the Vaal in forcing Pretoria's regime to the negotiating table. But they signified a triumphalist narrative of key events, beginning with the Treaty of Vereeniging of 1902 and ending with the signing of the constitution in 1996. A serious engagement with the meaning and content of the protests of 1984 and its legacy was largely absent.

The continuous trend to flatten the complexities of the past and to produce statist and triumphalist narratives obscures the ongoing struggles of a great majority of South Africans for a "better life for all". The trivialisation of past injustice by those who refuse to acknowledge that apartheid as a system was indeed a crime against humanity underpinned by structural and routine violence, has contributed towards an ahistorical understanding of contemporary struggles and a dangerous denial of the legacy of racism and inequality. Conversely, the triumphalist struggle narrative that has emerged equally obscures the ambiguities and multi-faceted layers of the struggle against white minority rule.

Vergangenheitsbewältigung requires space for the diverse stories Ndebele was anticipating in the late 1990s and an empathetic engagement with the different experiences and subjectivities racial segregation and the struggle against it produced.[22] As Antjie Krog poetically proclaims, 'You should imagine yourself through me and I myself through you'.[23] It also requires taking seriously the content of discourse past struggles produced: how individuals and groups envisaged, conceptualised and imagined freedom and democracy warrants sustained attention. As Ingrid de Kok pointed out, the aim is not to '"resolve" the turbulence, but to recompose it'.[24] While South Africa's virtual and physical landscape is inscribed with material and non-material sites of memory, legibility of these sites remains compartmentalised and meanings contested.[25] The burden of remembering the complexities of a painful past and the historical production of processes of inclusion and exclusion poses particular challenges to the project of nation-building in South Africa. As Neville Alexander pointed out, one of the greatest challenges is to 'remember without constantly rekindling the divisive passions of the past'.[26]

1   I have borrowed the concept of 'reluctant bonds' from Njabulo Ndebele to indicate the uneasy relations between different sections of society. See Njabulo Ndebele, 'The Lion and The Rabbit', in *Fine Lines from the Box*, ed. Njabulo Ndebele (Roggebaai: Umuzi, 2007), 115. I wish to thank Nadira Omarjee, Andile Magengelele, Rita Kesselring and Pascal Schmid for reading and commenting on the draft.

2   This short essay was inspired by a course Patrick Harries taught in 2005 on Public History, Heritage and Commemoration and his reflections on the term *Vergangenheitsbewältigung*.

3   This definition is taken from the Duden. See *Duden: Deutsches Universalwörterbuch*, s.v. 'Vergangenheitsbewältigung', accessed 14 December 2014, www.duden.de/recht schreibung/Vergangenheitsbewaeltigung

4   Deborah Posel, 'The TRC Report. What Kind of History? What Kind of Truth?' in *Commissioning the Past. Understanding South Africa's Truth and Reconciliation Commission*, ed. Deborah Posel and Graham Simpson (Johannesburg: Wits University Press, 2002), 149.

5   Posel, 'The TRC Report', 168.

6   I use the term 'black' as a political term to refer to all those who were oppressed under apartheid legislation.

7   Gabeba Baderoon, *Regarding Muslims. From Slavery to Post-Apartheid* (Johannesburg: Wits University Press, 2014), 29.

8   Patrick Harries, 'From Public History to Private Enterprise. The Politics of Memory in the New South Africa', in *Historical Memory in Africa. Dealing with the Past, Reaching for the Future in an Intercultural Context*, ed. Mamadou Diawara, Bernard Lategan and Jörn Rüsen (New York: Berghahn, 2010), 123.

9   Saul Dubow's recent book discusses the complexity of apartheid. See Saul Dubow, *Apartheid 1948–1994* (Oxford: Oxford University Press, 2014).

10   This definition is taken from the Oxford Dictionary. See *Concise Oxford English Dictionary*, 12th ed., s.v. 'empathy'.

11   On the role of history and memory in post-apartheid South Africa, see for example Annie Coombes, *History after Apartheid. Visual Culture and Public Memory in a Democratic South Africa* (Johannesburg: Wits University Press, 2004) and Hans Erik Stolten, ed., *History Making and Present Day Politics. The Meaning of Collective Memory in South Africa* (Uppsala: Nordiska Afrikainstitutet, 2007).

12   Although the contemporary use of racial categories, as defined the Population Registration Act of the 1950s, remains problematic and loaded with political sensitivities, race as a 'social construct' underpinned by material reality and subjectivity retains relevant. See Neville Alexander,

'On "race" in South Africa', in *Thoughts on the New South Africa*, ed. Neville Alexander (Johannesburg: Jacana, 2013), 115–31.

13   Institute for Justice and Reconciliation, *SA Reconciliation Barometer 2014. Reflecting on Reconciliation. Lessons from the Past, Prospects for the Future* (Institute for Justice and Reconciliation, 2014). Accessed 16 December 2014, http://reconciliationbarometer.org/wp-content/uploads/2014/12/IJR-SA-Reconciliation-Barometer-Report-2014.pdf, 32.

14   T. O. Molefe, 'Reconciliation Ideology or why I will not let Adriaan Vlok wash my feet', accessed 16 December 2014, http://reconciliationbarometer.org/2014/07/t-o-molefe-on-reconciliation-ideology/

15   Harries, 'From Public History to Private Enterprise', 137.

16   Jacob Dlamini recently published his book addressing the complex issue of betrayal and collaboration. See Jacob Dlamini, *Askari. A Story of Collaboration and Betrayal in the Anti-Apartheid Struggle* (Johannesburg: Jacana, 2014).

17   Njabulo Ndebele, 'The Triumph of Narrative', in *Fine Lines from the Box*, 91.

18   Franziska Rüedi, 'Political Mobilisation, Violence and Control in the Townships of the Vaal Triangle, South Africa, c.1976–1986 (DPhil thesis, University of Oxford, 2013).

19   Mondli Makhanya, '1984: A Bygone Year', *City Press*, 9 September 2014.

20   Gabeba Baderoon, 'Remembering Slavery in South Africa', *Africa is a Country*, 7 December 2014, accessed 11 December 2014, http://africasacountry.com/remembering-slavery-in-south-africa/.

21   Greg Marinovich, 'Sebokeng: The Lessons of 1984', *Daily Maverick*, 30 November 2012.

22   For analyses of the psychological implications of racism and racial segregation, see Garth Stevens, Norman Duncan and Derek Hook, ed., *Race, Memory and The Apartheid Archive. Towards a Psychosocial Praxis* (Johannesburg: Wits University Press, 2013).

23   Antjie Krog, *A Change of Tongue* (Cape Town: Random House Struik, 2009. Kindle Edition).

24   Ingrid de Kok, 'Cracked Heirlooms. Memory on Exhibition, in *Negotiating the Past. The Making of Memory in South Africa*, ed. Sarah Nuttall and Carli Coetzee (Cape Town: Oxford University Press, 1998), 61.

25   Harries, 'From Public History to Private Enterprise', 121.

26   Neville Alexander, 'The Politics of Reconciliation', in *An Ordinary Country: Issues in the Transition from Apartheid to Democracy in South Africa*, ed. Neville Alexander (New York: Berghahn, 2003), 117.

Veit Arlt

South African Jazz: The Basel Connection

Jazz has played an important role in the history of South Africa, and since the mid-twentieth century, the country probably features the strongest jazz scene on the continent.[1] The jazz that was created in places such as Sophiatown in the 1950s was part of a lively African urban culture. It was progressive and cosmopolitan in its out-look taking the Harlem Renaissance as a point of reference and source of inspiration. Jazz then was a means to express the aspirations of the disenfranchised population, and to assert humanity in a dehumanising environment.[2] If the 1950s were the high time of the swinging and stomping township jazz, the 1960s saw young musicians pushing the limits of their music, developing cutting-edge, radical sounds. The tight-ening of the apartheid system, the limits set to their development and interracial co-operation and the constant harassment by the authorities drove a great number of musicians into exile. Sathima Bea Benjamin, Dollar Brand (Abdullah Ibrahim), Johnny Dyani, Mongezi Feza, Johnny Geertze, Chris McGregor, Makaya Ntshoko, Dudu Pukwana, Miriam Makeba, Hugh Masekela, Louis Moholo and Philip Tabane are just some of those who were part of this first wave of exiled musicians. With an enormous energy based on the experience of apartheid and exile these South African jazz artists fuelled the international jazz scene, most especially free jazz. Unfor-tunately many of them perished in that creative fire.

In the 1990s jazz again provided the sound track to the making of the new South Africa. While the African Jazz Pioneers toured internationally as cultural ambassadors transporting an ever catchy jive based on the music of the 1950s, musicians from a new generation were again exploring new ways of interpreting South African Jazz, and in places such as the Bassline in Melville[3] they created new sounds for a new South Africa: Zim Ngqawana, Andile Yenana, Feya Faku, Moses Molelekwa, Sipho Gumede, Gito Baloi, Vusi Mahlasela, Louis Mhlanga, Carlo Mombelli, Marcus Wyatt, Mac McKenzie, Hilton Schilder, McCoy Mrubata or Paul Hanmer are some of the musicians who are emblematic for a scene that has consistently developed South African jazz further. They explored the meaning of jazz and the country's rich musical heritage in new and diverse ways, challenging conventions and experimenting with formats. This resulted at instances in fusion, cross-over and avant-garde jazz. In con-trast to this rich and dynamic scene, the international music market is largely domi-nated by a few well established artists from the first generation of exiled musicians. Top scorers are the late Miriam Makeba, Hugh Masekela and Abdullah Ibrahim, whereas the truly dynamic current generation of South African artists hardly gets the

The late Robbie Jansen (saxophone) with Mac McKenzie performing in one of the unforgettable early shows in the series. Picture: Katrin Kusmierz, 30 October 2004.

international attention it deserves.[4] Basel, however, has become one of the few places worldwide where the new South African jazz scene regularly receives exposure. The Basel audience indeed has acquired a taste and understanding for contemporary jazz from the Cape.

Celebrating 2004 with South African jazz

The celebration of the first decade of democracy in South Africa in 2004 offered an occasion to run a series of concerts with South African Jazz at the Bird's Eye jazz club—the first address for jazz lovers in Basel—in cooperation with the Centre for African Studies Basel. The Bird's Eye audience was thrilled by the performances of the Bheki Mseleku Quintet (with Feya Faku, Enoch Mthalane, Bongani Sokhela and Lulu Gontsana), Sean Bergin's Nansika from the Netherlands paying an emotional tribute to the music of Pukwana, Dyani, McGregor and Abdullah Ibrahim and, finally, a Cape Jazz outfit featuring Robbie Jansen, Mac McKenzie, Hilton Schilder, Steven Erasmus and Jack Momple. This first series of concerts quite naturally developed into a continuous flow of South African musicians to Basel and today the Bird's Eye has made a name for itself in South Africa. Numerous are the requests of South African jazz artists to perform here. For some of these artists, Basel became the stepping stone on their way to the heaven of free jazz—the Jazz Festival Willisau. This was the case with the late Zim Ngqawana who recorded his CD *Zimology Quartet: Live at Bird's Eye, Switzerland*[5] in 2007.

The residencies of South African artists also involve cooperation with students of
Jazz School Basel: Siya Makuzeni (vocals), Kaspar von Grünigen (bass) and Daniel Mudrack (drums).
Picture: Veit Arlt, May 2006.

Exchange and cooperation

Feya Faku became the first artist in residence in 2006—an idea that goes back to the
late drummer Lulu Gontsana. On the occasion of the very first concerts I organised
with the Bheki Mseleku Quintet in April 2004 Lulu voiced his wish to spend some
time in Basel to develop his ideas. Unfortunately he passed away just when the
necessary funds had been raised. However, since then the residencies have developed
into an institution and, besides Feya Faku, Siya Makuzeni, Hilton Schilder, Carlo
Mombelli, Marcus Wyatt, Bokani Dyer and Herbie Tsoaeli have had the opportunity to stay for one to two months in Basel, cooperate with both young and established musicians, develop new ideas and record their music. These encounters have
in turn resulted in lasting cooperation, friendship and visits of Swiss musicians to
South Africa. One of the most astonishing results from these activities has been the
Goema Symphony composed by Mac McKenzie. Mac's fame is grounded in the
legendary rock outfit the Genuines and later the jazzy Goema Captains. This band
translated the sound and rhythm of the Cape Town Carnival into new idioms and
took it—in Mac's words—'to the penthouse'. The Cape Town Carnival finds its roots
in the Cape slave culture, which later became the basis for the local working class
culture. In 2005 the time had come to take it yet to another level—the symphonic
concert hall. It was in Basel that Mac got the first opportunity to present his new
music, first with a jazz outfit, later to be enlarged by a string section and, finally a
Friendship Orchestra. Today he runs regular series of concerts with the Cape Town

Mac McKenzie presents his Goema Symphony No. 1 at the SABC Auditorium in Cape Town.
The project has its origins in Basel. Picture: John Edwin Mason, March 2011.

Goema Orchestra at the SABC studio. Through his Cape Town Composers' Work-shop other musicians, both young and established, receive the opportunity to present their works for and with this orchestra. On the basis of these activities Mac became the main character in the award-winning documentary *Mama Goema—the Cape Town Beat in Five Movements*.[6]

Creating a sense of home and humanity

In Cape Town the carnival and the music based on the traditions of the Cape slaves have become the means to create a sense of humanity in the harsh Cape Flats where a huge part of the Cape Town populace was relocated. Music has helped re-assert the right of the people of the Flats to the inner city.[7] The captivating beat today labelled as Goema has not only become a key element in creating Cape identity among the coloured, it is a sound and feeling that nurtures a sense of place and speaks to Cape-tonians far and wide. Much as was the case with Sophiatown jazz in the 1950s or with Goema in contemporary Cape Town, the jazz from South Africa has contributed to making Basel a homely place for a good number of South Africans[8]—among them Patrick Harries. And this is no coincidence as all these activities too go back to an instance of "reading Patrick Harries". In 2002 I had just finished my first music project labelled West African Pop Roots, which featured palm wine music from Ghana, when, after a talk at the Institute of Social Anthropology, we had a beer at the restaurant Zum Isaak on Münsterplatz. We were deliberating how we could contribute to the upcom-ing 10th anniversary of South Africa's new constitution when Patrick observed: 'You should once do a project like this (i.e. the West African Pop Roots programme) with Jazz from South Africa'. It was indeed this remark which triggered it all. Therefore,

The 2007 concert of the Zimology Quartet was the occasion for an encounter of three legendary artists: the late Zim Ngqawana (right), the drummer Makaya Ntshoko (left) and the late writer Lewis Nkosi (centre). Picture: Veit Arlt, April 2007.

besides his great contribution to the making of African History and African Studies in Basel, and his guidance and supervision of our projects, we have to thank Patrick for his encouragement to pursue cultural activities and the resulting deep encounters we have had with musicians from South Africa.

1 David Coplan, *Township Tonight! South Africa's Black City Music and Theatre*, 2nd ed. (Chicago: Chicago University Press, 2008); Gwen Ansell, *Soweto Blues: Jazz, Popular Music and Politics in South Africa* (New York: Continuum, 2005).

2 Coplan, *Township Tonight!*, 11.

3 The sampler *Live at the Bass Line* released in 1998 (Sheer Music SSPCD 008) is representative of that scene and moment.

4 Philip B. Songa: The Life and Times of South African Jazz. www.allaboutjazz.com/southafrica/lifetimes.htm (Accessed 31.12.2004).

5 Zimology Quartet. 2007. *Zimology Quartet: Live at Bird's Eye, Switzerland.* Ingoma Publishing ZIMCD001.

6 Calum MacNaughton, Ángela Ramirez and Sara Gouveia (directors). 2011. *Mama Goema—the Cape Town Beat in Five Movements.* 60min.

7 John Edwyn Mason, *One Love, Ghoema Beat: Inside the Cape Town New Year's Carnival* (Cape Town: Random House Struik, 2010); Denis-Constant Martin, *Coon Carnival: New Year in Cape Town, Past and Present* (Cape Town: David Philip Publishers, 1999).

8 The most prominent South African of Basel was the late writer Lewis Nkosi, who spent the last 12 years of his life in Basel. Lewis died in September 2010. For Lewis, exile had become a life condition from 1960 onward. One seminal text by Lewis on the topic of exile is 'Jazz in Exile' published in *Transition*, No. 24 (1966), pp. 34–37. The importance of South African jazz in Basel and its meaning for Nkosi is evident in his review of the concert by Zim Ngqawana's Zimology Quartet in April 2007, published in this volume.

The Duo RockArt of the late Alex van Heerden (accordion and trumpet, loopstation and effects) and Hilton Schilder (piano, uhadi and guitar) was one of the most innovative and exciting outfits the new South Africa has to offer. Picture: Katrin Kusmierz, 26 June 2005.

Chronology of South African jazz artists at the Bird's Eye

2004 Bheki Mseleku Quintet, Sean Bergin's Nansika, Robbie Jansen and the Sons of Table Mountain

2005 Cape Jazz and Duo RockArt (Hilton Schilder and Alex van Heerden)

2006 Residency of Feya Faku and Siya Makuzeni, Swiss tour of the Swiss South African Jazz Quintet, Mac McKenzie and the Goema Captains of Cape Town and Duo RockArt

2007 Beat Bag Bohemia, Tutu Puoane Quartet, Duo RockArt, Zimology Quartet, Paul van Kemenade Quintet—the South African Connection, Mac McKenzie and the Goema Captains of Cape Town, South African tour of the Swiss South African Jazz Quintet, residency of Makaya Ntshoko at the District Six Museum in Cape Town

2008 Paul Hanmer (piano solo), Residency of Hilton Schilder in Basel, Hilton Schilder and the Iconoclast, South Easter Project, Duo RockArt, Zimology Quartet, Rogue State Alliance, Beat Bag Bohemia, Swiss South African Jazz Quintet, Feya Faku Quintet (including recording), Symposium Ten Years of Hip Hop and Jazz. Cooperation and Exchange by Pro Helvetia Cape Town

Marcus Wyatt (trumpet), artist in residence at the Bird's Eye jazz club, and Fabian Gisler (bass) improvising in the installation Pebbles by Cape Town artist Justin Fiske, who at the time was in residence at the Basel Museum of Cultures. Picture: Veit Arlt, 15 May 2012.

2009 A Tribute to Alex van Heerden, Paul Hanmer and McCoy Mrubata Duo, Hilton Schilder and the Iconoclast, Mac McKenzie and the Goema Captains of Cape Town, Master Class of Ayanda Sikade with Makaya Ntshoko in Basel, Carlo Mombelli and the Prisoners of Strange, exercise course New Music in Africa

2010 Residency of Carlo Mombelli Mac McKenzie; Kyle Shepherd Quartet; Udai Mazumdar and Derek Gripper (tour and recording in South Africa)

2011 Tutu Puoane Sextet; Beat Bag Bohemia; Udai Mazumdar and Derek Gripper (tour in Switzerland); Paul Hanmer Quartet; Mac McKenzie's Goema Ensemble

2012 Residency of Marcus Wyatt; Mac McKenzie and the Friendship Orchestra; Kesivan Naidoo and the Lights, Carlo Mombelli; Kyle Shepherd Trio

2013 Hilton Schilder and The Iconoclast, Feya Faku Quintet (including a studio recording), Carlo Mombelli and the Prisoners of Strange European Edition (including a studio recording), Marcus Wyatt Quartet

2014 Paul Hanmer, the Rainmakers, Derek Gripper, Bokani Dyer Quintet, residency of Herbie Tsoaeli

2015 The Rainmakers, Dominic Egli's Pluralism, Black Box, Carlo Mombelli, Bokani Dyer Quintet, residency of McCoy Mrubata, Marcus Wyatt Quartet

Lewis Nkosi[1]

Concert Review: Zim Ngqawana at the Bird's Eye jazz club, 27–28.04 2007

'South Africans are coming!' is now the usual cry in jazz circles of this middle-sized Swiss town whenever our musicians are billed to play at the famous Basel jazz club, the Bird's Eye, on Kohlenberg Street. Our musicians first came here during the dark days of apartheid and they still keep coming. In the 1960s Abdullah Ibrahim was for some years resident pianist at the Atlantis, just down the street from the Bird's Eye, and returns every year for a concert—*in memoria*, as it were. Another musician who has served time—is that the right expression?—is Makaya Ntshoko, who sometimes accompanied Ibrahim on drums, and is still here minding the store. Recently the drummer formed his own jazz group that he named nostalgically *Makaya's New Tsotsis.*

As far as I know, there are no *tsotsi* in this pleasant Swiss town which lies at the very crossroads of three countries in Europe—Switzerland, Germany and France—except, of course, but who knows! Basel has played host to some dubious characters, including the great German philosopher, Friedrich Nietzsche, who finally went mad some years before he died. Nietzsche was for ten years professor of Philology at The University of Basel; sadly he attempted to find a wife here but 'to no avail'. So the story goes! This is surprising since, apart from being one of the friendliest towns, Basel also contains some of the most marriageable women in Europe.

In recent years Basel has played host to world musicians of every ilk, from Japanese virtuoso violinists to American jazz musicians like John Marsalis or Sonny Rollins; but the South Africans are great favourites, with the likes of Miriam Makeba, Bheki Mseleku, Mac McKenzie's Cape Jazz, and Robbie Jansen beating a well-trodden path to the headwaters of the Rhine. They have been celebrating anything from township jazz, District Six carnival music, and the rarely heard sounds of the San Rock Art group.[2] We were just getting ready to commemorate South Africa's National Freedom Day in Bern, while awaiting the arrival of Dee Dee Bridgewater and her Mali-Jazz Orchestra, when the cry was heard once again 'The South Africans are coming!' This was to announce the arrival of the most astonishingly innovative jazz from South Africa Basel has heard for a long time. The Port Elizabeth-born Zim Ngqawana, described in the Bird's Eye newsletter as 'probably one of the most progressive and versatile musicians to emerge from the new South Africa', brought his quartet into town at the end of April. Performing on a variety of instruments that featured him on alto-tenor sax, flute, *mbira* and mouth concertina,[3] during the evening's activities Ngqawana led his quartet through compositions based on South African traditional and township jazz, from AmaPondo laments to District Six carnival dance music. Along the way you could hear the grunting of *gida* dance music, to moans of the mouth concertina and xylophone which brought back the memory of all those familiar childhood sounds which used to fill train coaches transporting mine workers to and from Johannesburg.

As South African jazz-lovers probably know, Ngqawana is so multi-talented, a man of so many parts, that trying to pin him down to any single role, is nearly futile. But he is encouraged in his irrepressible mischief by a trio of three extremely gifted musicians, from bass-player Herbie Tsoaeli and Ayanda Sikade on drums, to the back-scratching collusion of his pianist Nduduzo Makhathini, one of the most bracing, if not abrasive, jazz pianists to emerge from South Africa in the 1990s. Nduduzo had already been here before, scaring the daylights out of the Swiss with clusters of chords and runs on the keyboard that can evoke at will Monk or Abdullah Ibrahim, not to mention all his other American jazz mentors. This makes for a repertoire which is a ceaseless exploration of anything from European classics to Indian musical idioms. Above all, these guys are endowed with a formidable energy. They are totally driven. The energy is effusive but finally not wasteful. As the first set wears on without a break no one knows how it will all end. After repeated mauling of the piano for over an hour a Swiss woman said: 'Someone is going to have to pay for retuning that piano!'

The man who is chiefly responsible for bringing out here most of our experimental musicians is of course Veit Arlt, a researcher at the Centre for African Studies Basel who also doubles up as the musically sensitive impresario[4] at the Bird's Eye. Arlt travels often to South Africa where he spends his time listening to the newest sounds.

1   This review was written by the late Lewis Nkosi at Basel for an unidentified South African Newspaper and is dated 10.05.2007. It is published here courtesy of Nkosi's partner Astrid Starck. Basel had become the writer's temporary home in the later part of his life. He stayed in an apartment overlooking the river Rhine and was a frequent visitor to the Bird's Eye jazz club.
2   Nkosi refers to the Duo RockArt composed of Hilton Schilder and the late Alex van Heerden.
3   The harmonica or mouth organ in South Africa is at times referred to as 'bone mouth' concertina.
4   The artistic director of the jazz club is its founder Stephan Kurmann. Veit Arlt, coordinator of the Centre for African Studies Basel, assists in programming South African artists at the club and organising residencies.

Stephanie Bishop

The Game Plan for a Successful Career

I am teaching a writing class at the University of Basel for the second time. Except for one, the students are non-Swiss, like me. They have been writing recently (and unprompted) about what it feels like to start an international career—about re-learning who we are in a different culture, the geography of the city and the geography of our own minds. One of the younger ones writes with some worry about whether she is making choices consistent with a strategic game plan for a woman in her early twenties. She is studying what interests her, but frets about where it will lead.

Indeed, it is hard to predict where our careers and our academic interests will take us. I moved to Basel in 2007 for the MA in African Studies program. I didn't know anyone there and I didn't know there wouldn't be snow. The fact that I dreaded even making telephone calls to persons unknown didn't seem grounds to not move across the world sight unseen, but if I had known about the snow I might have reconsidered; that's how I made career decisions, and this particular decision struck people as unconventional at best. I imagined this move at the time like a holding pattern for a flight waiting to land. The destination was clear: Grownupsville. But, due to poor weather and, you know, congestion, I needed to fly in circles until visibility cleared and I could make my grand arrival. A master's degree was my holding pattern on my way to a grown up career in something interesting—which I would, you know, sort out later.

My first day in Basel, I walked from the lunchtime welcome reception at the Centre for African Studies to the Kollegienhaus with a small group of new students and Patrick Harries, for my very first class—a lecture course on the History of Labour in South Africa, taught by Patrick. As cyclists zipped past us on the street, Patrick told us we 'must wear a helmet' if we planned on cycling around town. I didn't plan to cycle: helmets ruin hairdos, and besides that, I worried about trams. But who was this professor with the elegant English giving me parental safety talks five minutes after meeting me? I also heard Patrick was in a German class, and just one level above my own beginner class. I wondered how long he had been in Basel himself, how he ended up there, whether *he* had known in advance there wouldn't be snow. I didn't ask, because that was akin to calling strangers.

I surmised, however, from the fact that 15 of us had to sit on the floor of the classroom that Patrick was a popular lecturer. I got to class earlier after that, and from my comfortable seats in chairs I started to see why. Going to Patrick's class was going to hear a poignant story of intrigue and irony, empathetically told, and sometimes even illustrated live on overhead projector sheets. Some experienced lecturers have this magic ability to say interesting things, in no apparent rush, and with timing so precise that they have spun a cliff-hanger and uttered the words, 'And that's what we'll come back to after a seven minute break' just a hair before the bell chimes. Patrick has this skill. His thoughtful preparation was also evident in seminars, where I noticed how he anticipated what students might not already know. To clarify the term 'squatter' for a class discussing land rights, he demonstrated what it means 'to squat', literally, and from his squatted position beside the table elaborated the metaphor to land tenure.

He seemed infinitively more approachable after that.

Patrick's approachability, and particularly his interest in students as individuals, became more evident to me in the way he supervised my MA thesis. I went to see him to bemoan my dearth of good ideas for an MA topic. I shared a few possibilities that I thought could work, and then mentioned off-handedly that I have always been interested in 'boring things like road infrastructure and railway construction', though nothing like that was on my tentative list. He instantly perceived that these 'boring' infrastructure topics held a spark for me that was worth my time, and he suggested I look into water scarcity in South Africa. This affirmation of my interest—and Patrick's ability to spot it, tucked back among some weeds, as it were—set him apart as a teacher who listens well and is quick to encourage.

In other ways, too, Patrick has been a teacher who nudged me to grow professionally. There are some students who are a joy to teach. They get their work done on time, and it is thoughtful work. They step up to discussions, and never turn into mice when introduced to fancy professors visiting from the States. Then there are those other students—the ones who act like speaking loudly and slowly simultaneously is just another version of the trick where you're supposed to pat your head and rub your belly at the same time, while reciting the Declaration of Independence. Impossible feat. 'You aren't quite what we expect from Americans', Patrick told me once, as he tried to encourage me to boldly introduce myself to a guest speaker at a conference. 'They're usually a little more, ehm ...' and he hesitated, looking for the right adjective. 'Pushy?' I offered. 'Exactly', he said.

What I lacked in boldness of speech, I made up for in audacity regarding deadlines. In 2010, two days before the deadline to register for my MA thesis, I discovered that there was one teensy tiny problem, and that was that my points for my prerequisite seminar papers needed to first be registered. That is truly a small problem if one has actually written the papers and the professors have read them. It is a slightly larger problem if the classes took place a year ago, one paper is still unfinished and your professor is out of the country. Not one to be discouraged, I set to righting this muddle by emailing Patrick straight away. Would he be so kind as to read my seminar paper, all 30 pages of it, and enter the points within the next twenty-four hours? Even though he seemed to be away? Oh, and even though I would have to send the paper later, after I finished it? Patrick emailed me straight back, and with—I think we can agree on this—exceptional forbearance only said, 'Fortunately I am back from holiday so am in a good mood. Send it to me asap'.

When I moved to Basel I thought of it as a career holding pattern, turning circles until I could see where to land. But that is not quite right. One does not feel lost in a holding pattern, but we often do early in our careers as we find our way through unfamiliar space, literally and less literally. Instead of turning circles while we wait for an opportunity, a career path emerges out of the turns we make in response to those who invest in us—coaches who help us make up game plans on the fly, while we are still bundles of self-doubt and a pain in the neck. If it were not for my professors' good moods, I might never have graduated. Patrick's international career intersected mine in Basel in the first decade of mine and the last of his. His patient investment in my success and wellbeing since 2007 has been tremendously influential on my new career—it has framed my research topics, inspired my teaching style, and reassured me by way of example that moving across the world for work is not necessarily bat-crazy.

I visited my brother in New York before Christmas, and we went to a comedy cellar with a line-up of comedians in their late 20s, like us. Almost all of them had jokes about not feeling like adults, feeling that their careers aren't pulled together yet and having no real game plan to accomplish that. One said any time he clumsily spills a drink or knocks something off a table, before it hits the ground he has re-visited every failure of adulthood and it invariably ends with '... and I'll never be a homeowner'. I could relate, although for me, it tends to be triggered by things like snagging silk shirts, forgetting to return my library books, or painting my nails poorly. As I was procrastinating one week, searching the Internet for the courage to read a stack of my students' essays, I watched a Buzzfeed video called '12 Signs Being Ladylike is not Your Forté'.[1] One of those signs is that 'trying to paint your nails makes you wonder why anyone trusts you with anything', and the woman has painted not just her nail but the entire end of her finger red.

I think about this sometimes when I go in to teach my writing class and I see my name and my class details blinking on the wall in the main university building, indicating we're up. This announcement in English stands out among the German class announcements, and it makes me feel so grown up and far away. Except if I am under-prepared for class. Then I wonder, 'Do they know I've hardly written anything lately? Who let me in here? Should I even still live in Switzerland? If I keep this foreign thing up, I am never going to be a homeowner'. I have no game plan.

I have noticed, however, when I listen to more advanced academics who I know and admire—people such as Patrick—describe their career trajectories, it seldom seems they had one either. Yet, people trusted them with all kinds of things, and we have benefitted greatly.

One day when I had been in Basel about a month, I bumped into a friend in town. Could I call her a friend? I was impressed that people with whom I had not had a single person or place in common just a few short weeks before felt like friends, or at least like very positive connections who stopped to talk when they recognized me. Patrick was the first person in Switzerland to start calling me *Steph*, what my brothers and my friends in Oregon call me. He didn't ask if I had a preference for the long or short version of my name; he just switched, about the same time that he started sending me students who needed help with their writing. I wondered at the strange and surprising ways that a network—both professional and personal—springs up on a new landscape, like one great welcoming committee, and even gets your nickname right.

At the end of my first decade as an arguably productive member of society, I am starting to think that's how it is with careers: we set out not knowing quite where we are headed or how we will pull it off, and that feeling sticks. But with every turn there is someone to call us by name, model the skills we need, and prod us toward the next turn. During Patrick's time in Basel, he has certainly been that person for me in many instances. His work illustrates that a few decades of that—of being known, learning from others, and sharing what we have learned—all amount to quite a meaningful career in Grownupsville.

1 '12 Signs Being Ladylike is not Your Forté', YouTube-Video, 2:25, posted by BuzzFeedVideo, 11 February 2014, https://youtube.com/watch?v=mgOs3CDkbvQ

Notes on Contributors

Veit Arlt studied History and Geography at the University of Basel and earned his PhD with a thesis on the History of Ghana (*Christianity, Imperialism and Culture. The Expansion of the Two Krobo States, c.1830–1930* in 2005). He held the assistant's position in African History before he took on his current position as coordinator of the Centre for African Studies in 2007. He is also involved in event management and organizes concerts and workshops with African music linked to teaching and research activities at the Centre.

Stephanie Bishop completed an MA in African Studies in 2010 with a dissertation on mining and hydropolitics in South Africa, supervised by Patrick Harries. Stephanie is currently a research assistant and PhD student at the Centre for African Studies Basel. She studies water technology in Zambia as part of the research group investigating technological artefacts in african urban settings.

Melanie Eva Boehi holds an MA in history from the University of the Western Cape and has been a PhD candidate at the University of Basel since 2011. Her dissertation is concerned with the history of the South African botanical complex.

Gregor Dobler is professor for social anthropology at Freiburg University. He has published widely on France and Namibia, integrating historical research into anthropology. While teaching in Basel as a senior lecturer in anthropology from 2002 to 2010, he was a close colleague of Patrick Harries and a regular guest in the African History Department's Tuesday lectures. Frequent discussions on the relation between history and anthropology also led to a joint seminar on the topic. None of them has yet managed to completely convert the other.

Patrick Grogan is a PhD student in the Department of History at the University of Basel. After graduating with a BA in German Studies and History at Rhodes University, Grahamstown, South Africa in 2009, he completed his MA in African Studies at the University of Basel in 2012. Patrick Harries has supervised both his MA thesis on "'Improving' the Cape Colony, 1815–1821: The Perspectives of Sir Jahleel Brenton" and his on-going PhD dissertation on the history of early nineteenth century German naturalists at the Cape.

Tanja Hammel studied History and English Linguistics, Literature & Culture at the University of Basel and the University of Manchester. She is a PhD-student at the Basel Graduate School of History and an affiliated member of NCCR the Iconic Criticism. Her work in SNF-Project 146259, *Mary Elizabeth Barber (1818–1899): A History of Knowledge, Gender and Natural History* involved archival research in South Africa, England and Ireland as well as a research affiliation with the Department of History and the collaborative research project 'Race and Ethnicity in the Global South' at the University of Sydney, where her interest in gender history, visual history and the history of knowledge deepened.

Dag Henrichsen is a Namibian historian and archivist based at the Basler Afrika Bibliographien and the Department of History, University of Basel. He is the author of numerous publications and projects with regard to Namibian history and visuality as well as Southern African (acoustic) archive histories. With Patrick Harries he collaborated in the frame of various teaching and research activities throughout Patrick's time in Basel.

Paul Jenkins studied history and education at the University of Cambridge. From 1963 to 1972, he taught history at the University of Ghana. In 1972 he became an archivist at the Basel Mission. Concurrently, from 1989, he was a lecturer in African History at the University of Basel—and in this sense the immediate predecessor of Patrick Harries in Basel—as well as co-leader of bmpix.org, a project that improved the standards of conservation and access in the Basel Mission's collection of historical photographs. Since 2003 he has been working as a private scholar on the history of the Basel Mission in West Africa and India.

Rita Kesselring is a senior lecturer in Social Anthropology at the University of Basel. Her work concerns law, the body, memory, social change and methodology. Her regional focus is South Africa, Zambia and Southern Africa more general.

Cassandra Mark is currently a researcher and lecturer in African History at the University of Basel. She completed her doctorate at the University of Oxford in 2014. Her research interest lies in the social and economic history of West Africa. Themes running through her work include labour, urbanisation and transnational migration. She worked under Patrick Harries, then Chair of African History at the University of Basel, from August 2012 until December 2014.

Eric Morier-Genoud is a lecturer in African and Imperial History at Queen's University Belfast, United Kingdom. He has written extensively on religion and on politics in southern Africa. He is co-author of *Embroiled: Swiss Churches, South Africa and Apartheid* (2011), editor of *Sure Road? Nationalisms in Angola, Guinea-Bissau and Mozambique* (2012) and co-editor of *Imperial Migrations. Colonial Communities and Diaspora in the Portuguese World* (2012). He is also editor-in-chief of the journal *Social Sciences and Missions* (Leiden: Brill).

Franziska Rüedi holds an MA degree in African Studies from the University of Basel and a doctorate from the University of Oxford. She is currently a postdoctoral fellow at the University of the Witwatersrand. Her academic training was strongly influenced by Patrick Harries, whose courses she attended between 2001 and 2007. She worked as a student assistant and later as an assistant at the Chair of African History. Her current work focuses on political violence during the transition period in South Africa.

Pascal Schmid is a scientific collaborator at the Centre for African Studies Basel. From 2008 to 2011, he was a research assistant in the project History of Health Systems in Africa led by Patrick Harries. Under Patrick Harries' supervision, Pascal Schmid wrote his PhD thesis on the history of a former mission hospital and the development of health care services in rural Ghana.

Jürg Schneider is an historian affiliated with the Centre for African Studies, University of Basel, Switzerland. He has organized and curated various exhibitions. His writing on historical and contemporary African photography and photography in Africa appears in various journals and books. He co-initiated the project www.africaphotography.org, a platform for historical photographs from Africa, as well as www.african-photography-initiatives.org, a non-profit organization involved in various projects with the common goal of promoting Africa's rich photographic heritage.

Ulrike Sill is a theologian and historian. As a reverend minister in the Landeskirche Württemberg she set out to do her PhD in Theology at the University of Basel but eventually submitted her thesis in African History in 2007. Her study *Encounters in Quest of Christian Womanhood: The Basel Mission in Pre- and Early Colonial Ghana* was published in the Series *Studies in Christian Mission* (Brill 2010).

www.ingramcontent.com/pod-product-compliance
Lightning Source LLC
Chambersburg PA
CBHW080045280326
41935CB00014B/1789